THE
2000 CHARLTON
COIN GUIDE

39TH EDITION

Dealer's Buying Prices For
Canadian, Newfoundland and Maritime Coinage,
Canadian Medals, Tokens and Paper Money,
United States and World Gold Coinage

W. K. Cross
Publisher

The Charlton Press

Toronto, Ontario Birmingham, Michigan

COPYRIGHT AND TRADEMARK NOTICE

Canadian Cataloguing in Publication Data

The National Library of Canada has catalogued this publication as follows:

Charlton, J. E., 1911
    Charlton coin guide

18th ed. (1978)-
Continues: Charlton, J. E. 1911-   Coin guide of Canadian, Newfoundland and Maritime coinage.
ISSN 0706-0459
ISBN 0-88968-211-9 (39th ed.)

1. Coins, Canadian - Periodicals. 2. Coins - Prices - Periodicals. I. Title.

CJ1864.C5114   737.4' 9'71   C79-030323-X

**Printed in Canada
in the Province of Manitoba**

The Charlton Press

2040 Yonge Street, Suite 208, Toronto, Ontario. M4S 1Z9
Tel: (416) 488-1418 Fax: (416) 488-4656
Tel: (800) 442-6042 Fax: (800) 442-1542
www.charltonpress.comm e-mail Chpress@charltonpress.com

CONTENTS

INDEX OF DEALERS

INTRODUCTION

It is more difficult to obtain old coins in circulation, much more so than it was twenty-five years ago. For the most part silver no longer circulates, since its bullion value now exceeds its face value. Generally speaking, the only pre-1968 coins in circulation are one-cent and five-cent pieces, and these seldom pre-date 1953. Older coins must now be purchased through dealers.

BUYING AND SELLING PRICES

Buying prices are what dealers pay for coins. Selling prices are what dealers charge for coins. Generally, dealers will pay 40% to 60% of their selling price. It should be remembered all dealers will pay according to their needs. They will pay well for what they need immediately, but for those coins for which there is no demand, even if they have a high retail value, they will offer substantially less.

The prices shown in this book represent averages or estimates of buying prices and should serve as a guide in negotiating fair prices when buying or selling. Also a clearer idea of what coins are in demand by collectors and dealers can be developed by studying the guide.

Coins should not be mailed for appraisal unless a written response to an inquiry is received from the dealer. If coins are mailed, then they should be sent by registered mail, insured, accompanied by a list of the coins sent, with a complete return address and return postage.

HANDLING AND CLEANING COINS

Coins should be handled by the edges only. Avoid touching the surfaces. Many collectors have found too late that fingerprints cannot be removed from coins or other metal valuables. Proof and specimen quality coins must be handled with extra care since their high lustre is very fragile.

Inevitably, the question of whether to clean coins or not will arise. Probably the best course to follow is, when in doubt don't, until you have contacted an experienced collector or dealer.

The tarnish on silver coins can be removed, but it will not necessarily raise the value. If the tarnish is very thick, then its removal could leave the coin looking much worse.

Nickel coins seldom require cleaning, and only soap and water are safe since nickel is a fairly active metal. Copper and bronze should not be cleaned by anyone who is not knowledgeable in the chemical properties of these metals and their alloys.

Whatever the metal, abrasives must never be used. There are many polishes on the market which are designed for silverware, copper and brass. These must not be used with coins. The results are disastrous.

HANDLING AND CLEANING PAPER MONEY

Inexperienced collectors should always use great care when handling notes. Notes should be handled as little as possible, since oil and perspiration from one's skin can damage and devalue a note. Care should be taken to ensure that unfolded or uncreased notes remain so, and that even marginal tears or abrasions are avoided. Under no circumstances should one ever wash or otherwise try to clean a note since it is likely that the note's value will be considerably reduced. The same is true for ironing or pressing. It should be avoided.

MINT MARKS

A mint mark is a letter stamped on a coin to designate the mint that produced the coins.

Canadian decimal coinage issued prior to 1908 was struck at either the Tower Mint, London, in which case it had no mint mark, or at the Heaton Mint in Birmingham. The Birmingham coins have a small "H" as a mint mark. Since 1908 all Canadian coins have been struck at the Ottawa or Winnipeg Mints, with no mint marks, except the Canadian sovereigns which were identified by a small "C" above the date.

Newfoundland's coinage was struck at either London, Birmingham, or Ottawa. The Tower Mint coins had no marks, the Birmingham coins had an "H," and the Ottawa coins had a "C," except for the 1940 and 1942 cent pieces.

The coinage of New Brunswick and Nova Scotia had no mint marks because it was struck at the Tower Mint.

Prince Edward Island's coinage was struck at Birmingham, but no mint mark was used because the dies were supplied by the Tower Mint.

COINS OF CANADA

NOVA SCOTIA

VICTORIA 1861 - 1864

Date and Denomination	Buying Price
1861 half cent	3.00
1864 half cent	3.00
1861 one cent	1.25
1862 one cent	18.00
1864 one cent	1.25

PRINCE EDWARD ISLAND

VICTORIA 1871

Date and Denomination	Buying Price
1871 one cent	1.00

NEW BRUNSWICK

VICTORIA 1861 - 1864

Date and Denomination	Buying Price
1861 half cent	50.00
1861 one cent	1.25
1864 one cent	1.25
1862 five cents	30.00
1864 five cents	30.00
1862 ten cents	30.00
1864 ten cents	30.00
1862 twenty cents	15.00
1864 twenty cents	15.00

IMPORTANT: Buying prices are listed for coins graded VG or better. Bent, damaged or badly worn coins are not collectable and bring no premium value.

NEWFOUNDLAND

LARGE CENTS

Wide O   Narrow O

VICTORIA 1865 - 1896

Date and Mint Mark	Description	Buying Price
1865		1.50
1872H		1.50
1873		1.50
1876H		1.50
1880	Wide O	1.50
1880	Narrow O	80.00
1885		17.50
1888		17.50
1890		1.50
1894		1.50
1896		1.50

EDWARD VII 1904 - 1909

Date and Mint Mark	Buying Price
1904H	5.00
1907	1.00
1909	1.00

GEORGE V 1913 - 1936

Date and Mint Mark	Buying Price
1913	.50
1917C	.50
1919C	.50
1920C	.50
1929	.50
1936	.50

SMALL CENTS

GEORGE VI 1938 - 1948

Date and Mint Mark	Description	Buying Price
1938		.15
1940		.15
1940	Re-engraved Date	15.00
1941C		.15
1942		.15
1943C		.15
1944C		.15
1947C		.15

FIVE CENTS

VICTORIA 1865 - 1896

Date and Mint Mark	Buying Price
1865	20.00
1870	35.00
1872H	25.00
1873	50.00
1873H	750.00
1876H	60.00
1880	30.00

Date and Mint Mark	Buying Price
1881	18.00
1882H	18.00
1885	85.00
1888	25.00
1890	6.00
1894	6.00
1896	3.00

EDWARD VII 1903 - 1908

Date and Mint Mark	Buying Price
1903	1.50
1904H	1.50
1908	1.50

GEORGE V 1912 - 1929

Date and Mint Mark	Buying Price
1912	.75
1917C	.75
1919C	.75
1929	.75

GEORGE VI 1938 - 1947

Date and Mint Mark	Buying Price
1938	.75
1940C	.75
1941C	.75
1942C	.75
1943C	.75
1944C	.75
1945C	.75
1946C	200.00
1947C	.75

TEN CENTS

VICTORIA 1865 - 1896

Date and Mint Mark	Buying Price
1865	12.50
1870	140.00
1872H	12.50
1873	17.50
1876H	17.50
1880	25.00
1882H	12.50
1885	45.00
1888	12.50
1890	3.00
1894	3.00
1896	3.00

EDWARD VII 1903 - 1904

Date and Mint Mark	Buying Price
1903	2.00
1904H	1.50

GEORGE V 1912 -1919

Date and Mint Mark	Buying Price
1912	.45
1917C	.45
1919C	.45

IMPORTANT: Buying prices are listed for coins graded VG or better. Bent, damaged or badly worn coins are not collectable and bring no premium value.

8

GEORGE VI 1938 - 1947

Date and Mint Mark	Buying Price
1938	.45
1940	.45
1941C	.45
1942C	.45
1943C	.45
1944C	.45
1945C	.45
1946C	.45
1947C	.45

TWENTY CENTS

VICTORIA 1865 - 1900

Date and Mint Mark	Buying Price
1865	9.00
1870	15.00
1872H	6.00
1873	7.00
1876H	7.00
1880	8.00
1881	5.00
1882H	5.00
1885	6.00
1888	5.00
1890	4.00
1894	4.00
1896	4.00
1899	3.00
1900	3.00

EDWARD VII 1904

Date and Mint Mark	Buying Price
1904H	5.00

GEORGE V 1912

Date and Mint Mark	Buying Price
1912	.90

TWENTY-FIVE CENTS

GEORGE V 1917 - 1919

Date and Mint Mark	Buying Price
1917C	1.15
1919C	1.15

IMPORTANT: Mint marks are a letter stamped on a coin to designate the mint that produced the coin. The Canadian Mint used the letter "C," while the Heaton Mint in England used the letter "H."

IMPORTANT: Buying prices are listed for coins graded VG or better. Bent, damaged or badly worn coins are not collectable and bring no premium.

FIFTY CENTS

VICTORIA 1870 - 1900

Date and Mint Mark	Buying Price
1870	10.00
1872H	10.00
1873	30.00
1874	18.00
1876H	18.00
1880	18.00
1881	12.00
1882H	6.00
1885	7.00
1888	18.00
1894	2.25
1896	2.25
1898	2.25
1899	2.25
1900	2.25

GEORGE V 1911 - 1919

Date and Mint Mark	Buying Price
1911	2.25
1917C	2.25
1918C	2.25
1919C	2.25

TWO DOLLARS GOLD

VICTORIA 1865 - 1888

Date and Mint Mark	Buying Price
1865	175.00
1870	165.00
1872	250.00
1880	1,000.00
1881	125.00
1882H	125.00
1885	125.00
1888	125.00

EDWARD VII 1904 - 1909

Date and Mint Mark	Buying Price
1904H	2.25
1907	2.25
1908	2.25
1909	2.25

PROVINCE OF CANADA

LARGE CENTS

Wide 9 over 8	Narrow 9

VICTORIA 1858 - 1859

Date and Mint Mark	Description	Buying Price
1858		30.00
1859		1.00
1859	W/9 over 8	20.00

FIVE CENTS

Large date	Small date

VICTORIA 1858

Date and Mint Mark	Description	Buying Price
1858	Small Date	12.50
1858	Large Date	115.00

TEN CENTS

VICTORIA 1858

Date and Mint Mark	Buying Price
1858	15.00

TWENTY CENTS

VICTORIA 1858

Date and Mint Mark	Buying Price
1858	45.00

IMPORTANT: Buying prices are listed for coins graded VG or better. Bent, damaged or badly worn coins are not collectable and bring no premium value.

IMPORTANT: The buying prices for silver coins are based on their intrinsic value. All issues from 1902 to 1968 are priced at the market value for $7.50 (Can. funds) silver. Conditions play an important part in the buying price for coins between 1902 and 1936. Higher or lower silver prices will change the listed values.

DOMINION OF CANADA

LARGE CENTS

Large Date, Large Leaves

Small Date, Small Leaves

EDWARD VII 1902 - 1910

Date and Mint Mark	Buying Price
1902	.50
1903	.50
1904	.50
1905	.50
1906	.50
1907	.50
1907H	4.00
1908	.50
1909	.50
1910	.50

GEORGE V 1911 - 1920

Date and Mint Mark	Buying Price
1911	.20
1912	.20
1913	.20
1914	.20
1915	.20
1916	.20
1917	.20
1918	.20
1919	.20
1920	.20

VICTORIA 1876 - 1901

Date and Mint Mark	Description	Buying Price
1876H		1.00
1881H		1.00
1882H		1.00
1884		1.00
1886		1.00
1887		1.00
1888		1.00
1890H		3.00
1891	Large Leaves, Large Date	3.00
1891	Large Leaves, Small Date	40.00
1891	Small Leaves, Small Date	30.00
1892		1.00
1893		1.00
1894		1.00
1895		1.00
1896		1.00
1897		1.00
1898H		1.00
1899		1.00
1900		1.00
1900H		1.00
1901		1.00

Large cents were not issued for the years omitted in this listing.

IMPORTANT: Buying prices are listed for coins graded VG or better. Bent, damaged or badly worn coins are not collectable and bring no premium value.

SMALL CENTS

GEORGE V 1920 - 1936

Date and Mint Mark	Buying Price
1920 to 1921	.05
1922	6.00
1923	11.00
1924	3.00
1925	9.00
1926	1.00
1927 to 1929	.05
1930	.30
1931	.10
1932 to 1936	.05

1947 Maple Leaf

GEORGE VI 1937 - 1947

Date and Mint Mark	Description	Buying Price
1937 to 1947		.01
1947	Maple Leaf	.01

GEORGE VI 1948 - 1952

Date and Mint Mark	Description	Buying Price
1948	Without "ET IND:IMP"	.01
1949 to 1952		.01

No should fold   Shoulder Fold

ELIZABETH II 1953 - 1964

Date and Mint Mark	Description	Buying Price
1953	NSF	.01
1953	SF	.50
1954	NSF	100.00
1954	SF	.01
1955	NSF	50.00
1955	SF	.01
1956 to 1964		.01

Mature Head-Round   Centennial

ELIZABETH ii 1965 - 1981

Date and Mint Mark	Description	Buying Price
1965 to 1966		.01
1967	Centennial	.01
1968 to 1981		.01

Mature Head 12-sided

ELIZABETH II 1982 - 1989

Date and Mint Mark	Description	Buying Price
1982 to 1989		.01

Double Date

FIVE CENTS SILVER

1 9 0 0   1 9 0 0

1900 Small Date   1900 Large Date

1 8 7 4   1 8 7 4

Plain 4   Crosslet 4

ELIZABETH II 1990 to 1996

Date and Mint Mark	Description	Buying Price
1990 to 1991		.01
1992	Double Date	.01
1993 to 1996		.01

ELIZABETH II 1997 to 2000

Date and Mint Mark	Buying Price
1997 to 2000	.01

VICTORIA 1870 - 1901

Date and Mint Mark	Description	Buying Price
1870		7.00
1871		7.00
1872H		6.00
1874H	Plain 4	12.50
1874H	Crosslet 4	8.00
1875H	Large Date	85.00
1875H	Small Date	65.00
1880H		3.50
1881H		6.00
1882H		6.00
1883H		12.50
1884		85.00
1885		6.00
1886		6.00
1887		12.50
1888		3.50
1889		12.50
1890H		3.50
1891		3.50
1892		3.50
1893		3.50
1894		12.50
1896		3.50
1897		3.50
1898		6.00
1899		3.50
1900	Large Date	12.50
1900	Small Date	3.50
1901		3.50

Small H	Large H

EDWARD VII 1902 - 1910

Date and Mint Mark	Description	Buying Price
1902	Plain	1.00
1902	Large H	12.50
1902	Small H	4.00
1903		2.00
1903H		1.50
1904		1.50
1905		1.50
1906		1.50
1907		1.50
1908		1.50
1909		1.50
1910		1.50

GEORGE V 1911 - 1921

Date and Mint Mark	Buying Price
1911	.75
1912	.75
1913	.75
1914	.75
1915	3.00
1916	.75
1917	.75
1918	.75
1919	.75
1920	.75
1921	1,300.00

FIVE CENTS NICKEL

Near 6	Far 6

GEORGE V 1922 - 1936

Date and Mint Mark	Description	Buying Price
1922 to 1924		.07
1925		20.00
1926	Near 6	1.00
1926	Far 6	50.00
1927 to 1936		.07

Tombac Beaver	Tombac "V"

1947 Maple Leaf

GEORGE VI 1937 - 1952

Date and Mint Mark	Description	Buying Price
1937	Dot	.05
1938 to 1941		.05
1942	Nickel	.05
1942	Tombac Beaver	.15
1943	Tombac V	.07
1944 to 1945	Steel V	.10
1946 to 1947		.05
1947	Maple Leaf	.05

Geo. VI Obverse

Beaver

1951 High Relief

1951 Comm.

GEORGE VI 1948 - 1952

Date and Mint Mark	Description	Buying Price
1948	Without "ET IND:IMP"	.05
1949 to 1951		.05
1951	Commemorative	.05
1951	High Relief	200.00
1952		.05

ELIZABETH II 1953 - 1962

Date and Mint Mark	Buying Price
1953 to 1962	.05

ELIZABETH II 1963 - 1964

Date and Mint Mark	Buying Price
1963 to 1964	.05

Centennial

ELIABETH II 1965 - 1989

Date and Mint Mark	Description	Buying Price
1965 to 1966		.05
1967	Centennial	.05
1968 to 1989		.05

Double Date

ELIZABETH II 1990 - 2000

Date and Mint Mark	Description	Buying Price
1990 to 1991		.05
1992	Double Date	.05
1999 to 2000		.05

TEN CENTS

Flat Top 3   Round Top 3

VICTORIA 1870 -1901

Date and Mint Mark	Description	Buying Price
1870		12.00
1871		12.00
1871H		15.00
1872H		50.00
1874H		7.00
1875H		150.00
1880H		7.00
1881H		7.00
1882H		10.00
1883H		22.50
1884		135.00
1885		17.50
1886		12.00
1887		17.50
1888		6.00
1889		350.00
1890H		9.00
1891		9.00
1892		9.00
1893	Flat Top 3	7.00
1893	Round Top 3	400.00
1894		12.50
1896		6.00
1898		6.00
1899		6.00
1900		6.00
1901		6.00

EDWARD VII 1902 - 1910

Date and Mint Mark	Buying Price
1902	2.75
1902H	2.75
1903	3.00
1903H	2.75
1904	2.75
1905	2.75
1906	2.75
1907	2.75
1908	2.75
1909	2.75
1910	2.75

Small Leaves   Broad Leaves

GEORGE V 1911 - 1936

Date and Mint Mark	Description	Buying Price
1911		3.00
1912		.50
1913	Broad Leaves	75.00
1913	Small Leaves	.50
1914 to 1936		.50

GEORGE VI 1937 - 1947

Date and Mint Mark	Description	Buying Price
1937 to 1947		.35
1947	Maple Leaf	.35

17

Double Date

GEORGE VI 1948 - 1952

Date and Mint Mark	Description	Buying Price
1948	Without "ET IND"IMP"	.50
1949 to 1952		.35

ELIZABETH II 1953 - 1964

Date and Mint Mark	Description	Buying Price
1953 to 1964		.35

ELIZABETH 1990 - 2000

Date and Mint Mark	Description	Buying Price
1990 to 1991		.10
1992	Double Date	.10
1993 to 2000		.10

Centennial

1969 Small Date   1969 Large Date

ELIZABETH II 1965 - 1989

Date and Mint Mark	Description	Buying Price
1965 to 1966		.35
1967	Centennial	.35
1968	.500 Fine Silver	.30
1968	Nickel	.10
1969	Large Date	6,000.00
1969	Small Date	.10
1970 to 1989		.10

TWENTY-FIVE CENTS

Narrow O   Wide O

VICTORIA 1870 - 1901

Date and Mint Mark	Description	Buying Price
1870		7.00
1871		9.00
1871H		9.00
1872H		6.00
1874H		6.00
1875H		200.00
1880H	Narrow O	30.00
1880H	Wide O	85.00
1881H		9.00
1882H		9.00
1883H		7.00
1885		75.00
1886		9.00
1887		75.00
1888		12.00
1889		90.00
1890H		12.00
1891		40.00
1892		7.00
1893		75.00
1894		6.00
1899		6.00
1900		6.00
1901		6.00

EDWARD VII 1902 - 1910

Date and Mint Mark	Buying Price
1902	3.00
1902H	3.00
1903	5.00
1904	7.00
1905	5.00
1906	3.00
1907	3.00
1908	5.00
1909	3.00
1910	3.00

GEORGE V 1911- 1936

Date and Mint Mark	Description	Buying Price
1911		4.00
1912 to 1914		2.00
1915		7.00
1916 to 1920		2.00
1921		5.00
1927		12.00
1928 to 1936		2.00
1936	Dot	17.50

GEORGE VI 1937 - 1947

Date and Mint Mark	Description	Buying Price
1937 to 1947		.90
1947	Maple Leaf	.90

GEORGE VI 1948 - 1952

Date and Mint Mark	Descripton	Buying Price
1948	Without "ET IND:IMP"	.90
1949 to 1952		.90

1973 Small Bust
120 Obverse Beads
Far from Rim

1973 Large Bust
132 Obverse Beads
Near Rim

1974/89 Mature Head
Small Beads

Caribou.

ELIZABETH II 1953 - 1964

Date and Mint Mark	Description	Buying Price
1953	Large Date	.90
1953	Small Date	.90
1954 to 1964		.90

RCMP

ELIZABETH II 1973 - 1989

Date and Mint Mark	Description	Buying Price
1973	Small Bust	.25
1973	Large Bust	35.00
1974 to 1989		.25

Centennial

ELIZABETH II 1990 - 1991

Date and Mint Mark	Buying Price
1990	.25
1991	1.00

ELIZABETH II 1965 - 1972

Date and Mint Mark	Description	Buying Price
1965 to 1966		.90
1967	Centennial	.75
1968	.500 Fine Silver	.55
1968 to 1972	Nickel	.25

CANADA 125 ANNIVERSARY

Issued in 1992 to commemorate Canada's 125th birthday. The twelve different quarters represent images from the ten provinces and two territories. The composition is nickel.

Nova Scotia

Quebec

Common Obverse

Saskatchewan

British Columbia

New Brunswick

Northwest Territories

Newfoundland

Manitoba

ELIZABETH II 1992

Date and Mint Mark	Description	Buying Price
1992	New Brunswick	.25
1992	Northwest Territories	.25
1992	Newfoundland	.25
1992	Manitoba	.25
1992	Yukon	.25
1992	Alberta	.25
1992	Prince Edward Island	.25
1992	Ontario	.25
1992	Nova Scotia	.25
1992	Quebec	.25
1992	Saskatchewan	.25
1992	British Columbia	.25
1992	Double Date	2.00

Note: 1992 Caribou double date quarters found only in RCM sets.

Yukon

Alberta

Prince Edward Island

Ontario

ELIZABETH II 1993 - 1999

Date and Mint Mark	Description	Buying Price
1993 to 1996		.25
1997	1997 to 1999	2.00
1998	Caribou quarters found	2.00
1999	only in R.C.M. Sets	2.00

1999 MILLENNIUM QUARTERS

Issued to start the Millennium celebration, the following twelve quarters were released one per month during 1999. The obverse is as the 1993 issue.

November   December

January   February

March   April

May   June

July   August

September   October

ELIZABETH 1999

Date and Mint Mark	Description	Buying Price
1999	January	.25
1999	February	.25
1999	March	.25
1999	April	.25
1999	May	.25
1999	June	.25
1999	July	.25
1999	August	.25
1999	September	.25
1999	October	.25
1999	November	.25
1999	December	.25

2000 MILLENNIUM QUARTERS

Elizabeth 2000

Date and Mint Mark	Description	Buying Price
2000	January	.25
2000	February	.25
2000	March	.25
2000	April	.25
2000	May	.25
2000	June	.25
2000	July	.25
2000	August	.25
2000	September	.25
2000	October	.25
1999	November	.25
1999	December	.25

FIFTY CENTS

L.C.W.   No L.C.W.

VICTORIA 1870 - 1901

Date and Mint Mark	Description	Buying Price
1870	Without L.C.W.	450.00
1870	With L.C.W.	40.00
1871		55.00
1871H		55.00
1872H		35.00
1881H		35.00
1888		110.00
1890H		600.00
1892		35.00
1894		275.00
1898		35.00
1899		85.00
1900		27.50
1901		27.50

EDWARD VII 1902 - 1910

Date and Mint Mark	Buying Price
1902	7.00
1903H	12.00
1904	65.00
1905	65.00
1906	12.00
1907	7.00
1908	4.00
1909	4.00
1910	4.00

GEORGE V 1911 - 1936

Date and Mint Mark	Buying Price
1911 to 1920	3.50
1921*	8,000.00
1929	3.50
1931	7.00
1932	36.00
1934	10.00
1936	10.00

*Majority were melted down. Approximately 75 are known. Beware of altered date.

Straight "7" No Maple Leaf	Curved "7" No Maple Leaf

Staight "7" With Maple Leaf	Curved "7" With Maple Leaf

GEORGE VI 1937 - 1947

Date and Mint Mark	Description	Buying Price
1937 to 1946		1.80
1947	Straight "7"	1.80
1947	Curved "7"	1.80
1947	M.L., Straight "7"	12.00
1947	M.L., Curved "7"	675.00

GEORGE VI 1948 - 1952

Date and Mint Mark	Description	Buying Price
1948	Without "ET IND:IMP"	30.00
1949 to 1952		1.80

ELIZABETH II 1965 - 1967

Date and Mint Mark	Description	Buying Price
1965 to 1966		1.80
1967	Centennial	1.80

No shoulder fold   Shoulder fold

ELIZABETH II 1968 - 1989

Date and Mint Mark	Buying Price
1968 to 1989	.50

Small date   Large date

ELIZABETH II 1953 to 1964

Date and Mint Mark	Description	Buying Price
1953	SD, NSF	1.80
1953	LD, NSF	3.00
1953	LD, SF	1.80
1954 to 1964		1.80

ELIZABETH II 1990 - 2000

Date and Mint Mark	Description	Buying Price
1990 to 1991		.50
1992	Double date	.50
1993 to 1995		.50
1996 to 2000	Modified reverse	.50

SILVER DOLLARS

1935 Obverse

1936 Obverse

1937 to 1947 Obverse

1935 Reverse

1939 Parliament

1949 Newfoundland

$$1947 \quad 1947$$

Blunt 7   Pointed 7

1952 Water Lines   1952 No Water Lines

$$1947.$$

1947 Maple Leaf

GEORGE V 1935 - 1936

Date and Mint Mark	Description	Buying VF Price
1935	Silver Jubilee	15.00
1936	Voyageur	10.00

GEORGE VI 1937 - 1947

Date and Mint Mark	Description	Buying VF Price
1937	Voyageur	9.00
1938	Voyageur	25.00
1939	Royal Visit	4.00
1945	Voyageur	85.00
1946	Voyageur	20.00
1947	Blunt 7	50.00

GEORGE VI 1947 - 1952

Date and Mint Mark	Description	Buying VF Price
1947	Pointed 7	60.00
1947	Maple Leaf	80.00
1948	Dei Gratia	500.00
1949	Newfoundland	9.00
1950	Voyageur	6.00
1950	Arnprior	6.00
1951	Voyageur	5.00
1951	Arnprior	20.00
1952	Water Lines	5.00
1952	No Water Lines	5.00

Arnprior dollars are known to exist in the years 1950, 1951 and 1955. Other years may contain Arnprior varieties but are unknown at the present time.

1953 Obverse	1959 Reverse	1964 Charlottetown

1958 British Columbia	1965 Obverse	1967 Centennial

1955 4 Water Lines	1955 2 1/2 Water	1957 4 Water Lines	1957 2 1/2 Water

ELIZABETH II 1953 to date

Date and Mint Mark	Description	Buying VF Price
1953	Voyageur	3.50
1954	Voyageur	5.00
1955	Voyageur	5.00
1955 Arnprior	One waterline	35.00
1956	Voyageur	6.00
1957	Voyageur	3.50
1957 Arnprior	One Waterline	3.50
1958	British Columbia	3.50
1959	Voyageur	3.50

ELIZABETH II 1960 - 1967

Date and Mint Mark	Description	Buying VF Price
1960	Voyageur	3.50
1961	Voyageur	3.50
1962	Voyageur	3.50
1963	Voyageur	3.50
1964	Charlottetown	3.50
1965	Voyageur	3.50
1966	Voyageur	3.50
1967	Centennial	3.50

IMPORTANT: Do not clean your coins. Coins should be handled carefully. Only experts should consider cleaning. If you are not an expert, the results can be disastrous.

IMPORTANT: The silver dollar buying prices are for problem free coins in very fine condition. Damaged coins will bring lower prices.

NICKEL DOLLARS

Common Obverse

Voyageur Reverse

Manitoba

British Columbia

Prince Edward Island

Winnipeg

Constitution

Jacques Cartier

ELIZABETH II 1968 - 1974

Date and Mint Mark	Description	Buying Price
1968	Voyageur	1.00
1969	Voyageur	1.00
1970	Manitoba	1.00
1971	British Columbia	1.00
1972	Voyageur	1.00
1973	P.E.I.	1.00
1974	Winnipeg	1.00

ELIZABETH II 1957 - 1987

Date and Mint Mark	Description	Buying Price
1975 to 1981	Voyageur	1.00
1982	Constitution	1.00
1983	Voyageur	1.00
1984	Jacques Cartier	1.00
1985	Voyageur	1.00
1986	Voyageur	1.00
1987	Voyageur	1.00

NICKEL BRONZE DOLLARS

ELIZABETH II 1987 - 1989

Date and Mint Mark	Description	Buying Price
1987	Proof	2.00
1987 to 1989	Loon	1.00

ELIZABETH II 1992 - 1993

Date and Mint Mark	Description	Buying Price
1992	Double Date	1.00
1993	Loon	1.00

ELIZABETH II 1990 - 1991

Date and Mint Mark	Description	Buying Price
1990 to 1991	Loon	1.00

ELIZABETH II 1994

Date and Mint Mark	Description	Buying Price
1994	Remembrance Unc	1.00
1994	Remembrance Proof	5.00
1994	Loon	1.00

CANADA 125
Issued to commemorate the 125th birthday of Canada.

ELIZABETH II 1995 - 1996

Date and Mint Mark	Description	Buying Price
1995	Peacekeeping Unc	1.00
1995	Peacekeeping Proof	5.00

ELIZABETH II 1992

Date and Mint Mark	Description	Buying Price
1992	Unc	1.00
1992	Proof	4.00

Note: Proof issues of the 1987, 1992, 1994 and 1995 issue were issued by the Numismatic Department of the Royal Canadian Mint.

ELIZABETH II 1995 - 1997

Date and Mint Mark	Description	Buying Price
1995-1996	Loon	1.00
1997	Loon	2.00
1997	10th Anniversary	5.00
1997	10th Anniv. Silver	40.00

Note: The 1997 to 2000 one dollar loons were issued only in RCM sets.

ELIZABETH II 1998 - 2000

Date and Mint Mark	Description	Buying Price
1998	The 1997, 98, 99	2.00
1999	and 2000 one	2.00
2000	dollar Loons are	2.00

TWO DOLLAR COINS

ELIZABETH II 1996 - 1998

Date and Mint Mark	Description	Buying Price
1996	Circulating	2.00
1996	Proof	10.00
1996	Double thickness	50.00
1996	Gold	200.00
1997		2.00
1998		2.00

ELIZABETH II 1999 - 2000

Date and Mint Mark	Description	Buying Price
1999	Circulating	2.00
1999	Proof	10.00
1999	Gold	200.00
2000		2.00

GOLD COINS

SOVEREIGNS

EDWARD VII 1908 - 1910

Date and Mint Mark	Buying Price
1908C	1,100.00
1909C	150.00
1910C	135.00

GEORGE V 1911 - 1919

Date and Mint Mark	Buying Price
1911C	90.00
1913C	300.00
1914C	150.00
1916C	9,000.00
1917C	90.00
1918C	90.00
1919C	90.00

FIVE DOLLARS

GEORGE V 1912 - 1914

Date and Mint Mark	Buying Price
1912	135.00
1913	135.00
1914	225.00

TEN DOLLARS

GEORGE V 1912 - 1914

Date and Mint Mark	Buying Price
1912	275.00
1913	275.00
1914	300.00

TWENTY DOLLARS

ELIZABETH II 1967

Date and Mint Mark	Description	Buying Price
1967	Centennial	180.00
1967	Complete Set	190.00

IMPORTANT: Do not clean your coins. Coins should be handled carefully. Only experts should consider cleaning. If you are not an expert, the results can be disastrous.

COLLECTORS ISSUES

The numismatic department of the Royal Canadian Mint issued specially struck and packaged coins starting in 1954. The coins were issued for collectors and as a result are of high quality. The dealer buying prices listed below are for single coins and sets in their original packaging and condition. Coins or sets which have been mishandled or damaged are discounted from the prices listed. Beginning in 1971 the numismatic department of the Royal Canadian Mint issued silver dollars for collectors in two conditions, proof and uncirculated. Proof condition dollars were issued in black leatherette boxes while uncirculated dollars were issued in a clear plastic container.

SILVER TEN CENTS

500TH Anniversary of Caboto's First Transatlantic Voyage; 1997: Giovanni Caboto sailed from Bristol, England in 1497. Sighting "Newfoundland" weeks later he is credited with opening North America for settlement. The Matthew is depicted in full sail approaching the rocky coast of Newfoundland.
Buying Price: $5.00

SILVER TWENTY-FIVE CENTS

1992 - 125th ANNIVERSARY SILVER QUARTERS PROOF SET

Issued by the mint in 1992. The silver twenty-five cent coins were sold singly and in sets. The thirteen coins are twelve twenty-five cent coins and a dollar coin, and the set is housed in a blue presentation box. See page 21 for illustrations.
Buying Prices: Singly: $4.00   Set: $45.00

1999 MILLENNIUM SILVER QUARTERS PROOF SET

Again in 1999 the mint issued silver twenty-five cent coins. These were sold singly and in sets. Each were housed in presentation boxes. See page 22 for illustrations
Buying prices: Singly: $4.00   Set $45.00

SILVER FIFTY CENTS
WILD LIFE SERIES

| Atlantic Puffins | Gray Jays | White Tailed Ptarmigans | Whooping Crane |

Date	Description	Buying Price	Date	Description	Buying Price
1995	Atlantic Puffins	5.00	1995	White Tailed Ptarmigans	5.00
1995	Gray Jays	5.00	1995	Whooping Crane	5.00

| Black Bear Cubs | Cougar Kittens | Mouse Calf | Wood Ducklings |

Date	Description	Buying Price	Date	Description	Buying Price
1996	Black Bear Cubs	5.00	1996	Mouse Calf	5.00
1996	Cougar Kittens	5.00	1996	Wood Ducklings	5.00

| Canadian Eskimo Dog | Labrador Retriever | Newfoundland | Nova Scotia Duck Tolling Retriever |

Date	Description	Buying Price	Date	Description	Buying Price
1997	Canadian Eskimo Dog	5.00	1997	Newfoundland	5.00
1997	Labrador Retriever	5.00	1997	Nova Scotia Duck Tolling Retriever	5.00

WILDLIFE SERIES

| Beluga Whale | Blue Whale | Humpback Whale | Killer Whale |

Date	Description	Buying Price	Date	Description	Buying Price
1998	Beluga Whale	5.00	1998	Humpback Whale	5.00
1998	Blue Whale	5.00	1998	Killer Whale	5.00

| Tonkinese | Lynx | Cymric | Cougar |

Date	Description	Buying Price	Date	Description	Buying Price
1999	Tonkinese	5.00	1999	Cymric	5.00
1999	Lynx	5.00	1999	Cougar	5.00

SPORTS SERIES

| Auto Racing | Skating | Skiing | Soccer |

Date	Description	Buying Price	Date	Description	Buying Price
1998	Auto Racing	5.00	1999	Skiing	5.00
1998	Skating	5.00	1999	Soccer	5.00

SPORTS SERIES

Golf	Yacht Race	Basketball	Football

Photograph not available at press time (Basketball)

Photograph not available at press time (Football)

Date	Description	Buying Price	Date	Description	Buying Price
1998	Golf	5.00	1999	Basketball	5.00
1998	Yachting	5.00	1999	Football	5.00

SILVER PROOF-LIKE DOLLARS

Issued by the Royal Canadian Mint for collectors. Illustrations of these dollars can be found on pages 26 and 27.

Date	Description	Buying Price	Date	Description	Buying Price
1954	Voyageur	60.00	1959	Voyageur	5.00
1955	Voyageur	50.00	1960	Voyageur	5.00
1955	Arnprior	75.00	1961	Voyageur	3.50
1956	Voyageur	30.00	1962	Voyageur	3.50
1957	Voyageur	25.00	1963	Voyageur	3.50
1958	British Columbia	20.00	1964	Charlottetown	3.50

CASED NICKEL DOLLARS

Manitoba   British Columbia   Prince Edward Island

Winnipeg   Constitution   Jacques Cartier

Date	Description	Buying Price	Date	Description	Buying Price
1970	Manitoba	1.00	1975	Voyageur	1.00
1971	British Columbia	1.00	1976	Voyageur	1.00
1972	Voyageur	1.00	1982	Constitution	2.00
1973	Prince Edward Island	1.00	1984	Jacques Cartier	2.00
1974	Winnipeg	1.00			

CASED SILVER DOLLARS

Common Obverse

1971 British Columbia

1973 R.C.M.P.

1974 Winnipeg

1975 Calgary

1976 Parliament

1977 Jubilee

1978 Commonwealth

1979 Griffon

Date	Description	Buying Price	Date	Description	Buying Price
1971	British Columbia	5.00	1976	Library of Parliament	5.00
1972	Voyageur	5.00	1977	Jubilee	4.00
1973	R.C.M.P.	5.00	1978	Commonwealth Games	4.00
1974	Winnipeg	5.00	1979	Griffon	7.00
1975	Calgary Stampede	5.00			

CASED SILVER DOLLARS

1980 Arctic Territories

1981 Trans Canada

1982 Regina

1983 University Games

1984 Toronto

1985 National Parks

1986 Vancouver

1987 Davis Strait

1988 Ironworks

Date	Description	Buying Price	Date	Description	Buying Price
1980	Arctic Territories	15.00	1985	National Parks (PF)	6.00
1981	Trans Canada (PF)	11.00	1985	National Parks (UNC)	6.00
1981	Trans Canada (UNC)	5.00	1986	Vancouver (PF)	6.00
1982	Regina (UNC)	5.00	1986	Vancouver (UNC)	10.00
1982	Regina (PF)	4.00	1987	Davis Strait (PF)	8.00
1983	University Games (PF)	5.00	1987	Davis Strait (UNC)	6.00
1983	University Games (UNC)	4.00	1988	Ironworks(PF)	14.00
1984	Toronto (PF)	6.00	1988	Ironworks (UNC)	16.00
1984	Toronto (UNC)	8.00			

Note: (PR) Proof condition issued in a black leatherette case .
(UNC) Uncirculated condition issued in a clear plastic case.

CASED SILVER DOLLARS

1989 MacKenzie River

1990 Henry Kelsey

Common Obverse 1990 to date

1991 Frontenac

1992 Stagecoach

1993 Hockey

1994 R.C.M.P.

1995 325th Anniversary of
Hudson's Bay

1996 McIntosh 200th
Anniversary

Date	Description	Buying Price	Date	Description	Buying Price
1989	MacKenzie River (PF)	14.00	1993	Hockey (PF)	10.00
1989	MacKenzie River (UNC)	15.00	1993	Hockey (UNC)	6.00
1990	Henry Kelsey (PF)	12.00	1994	RCMP (PF)	15.00
1990	Henry Kelsey (UNC)	6.00	1994	RCMP (UNC)	12.00
1991	Frontenac (PF)	10.00	1995	Hudson's Bay (PF)	10.00
1991	Frontenac (UNC)	6.00	1995	Hudson's Bay (UNC)	6.00
1992	Stagecoach (PF)	10.00	1996	McIntosh (PF)	12.00
1992	Stagecoach (UNC)	6.00	1996	McIntosh (UNC)	8.00

Note: (PR) Proof condition issued in a black leatherette case .
(UNC) Uncirculated condition issued in a clear plastic case.

CASED SILVER DOLLARS

1997 Canada/Russia Hockey   125th Anniversary RCMP   1999 Juan Perez

Photograph
not
available
at press
time

Photograph
not
available
at press
time

1999 Older Persons   2000   2001

Date	Description	Buying Price	Date	Description	Buying Price
1997	Hockey (PF)	15.00	1999	Perez (PF)	15.00
1997	Hockey (UNC)	8.00	1999	Perez (UNC)	8.00
1998	RCMP (PF)	15.00	1999	Older Persons (PF)	15.00
1998	RCMP (UNC)	8.00	1999	Older Persons (UNC)	8.00

FIVE DOLLAR COIN

ELIZABETH II 1996

Date	Description	Buying Price
1996	Bethune	20.00

Note: (PR) Proof condition issued in a black leatherette case .
(UNC) Uncirculated condition issued in a clear plastic case.

START THE MILLENNIUM RIGHT
JOIN THE CNA.

Applications for membership in the Canadian Numismatic Association may be made by any reputable party upon payment of the required dues.

(check one of each group)

☐ New   ☐ Renewal ⎯⎯⎯⎯⎯⎯⎯   ☐ Reinstatement
                    (member number)

☐ Regular   ☐ Junior   ☐ Family

☐ Corporate   ☐ Life Membership

☐ Mr.   ☐ Mrs.   ☐ Ms.   ☐ Club

Name:

Street: *Address may be published in the Journal* ☐ *yes* ☐ *no*

City: *Province/State*   *Postal Code/Zip*

Country   *Birthdate*

Signature of applicant   *Signature of Sponsor*

Signature of guardian (if under 18 years of age)

Dues

Dues shown are in Canadian dollars to Canadian addresses and in U.S. dollars to all other addresses. Payment may be made by money order, bank draft or personal cheque. We regret that we are unable to offer credit card services. Postage stamps are not acceptable. Currency (U.S. or Canadian only) is acceptable and should be sent by security registered mail only. Membership is not Goods and Services taxable.

REGULAR* - Applicants 18 years of age or over **$33.00**

JUNIOR - Applicants under 18 years of age **$16.50**
        Persons under 18 must be sponsored by a parent or guardian

FAMILY - Husband, wife and children at home, under 18 years of age
        One Journal only **$44.00**

CORPORATE - Clubs, Societies, Libraries and other non-profit
        organizations **$33.00**

LIFE MEMBERSHIP **$495.00**

(After one year of regular membership. Details on payment plan available on request.)

First class mailing of the Journal is available on remittance of $9.00 (Cdn.) to Canadian addresses, $7.50 (U.S.$) to U.S.A. addresses and $15.00 (U.S.$) to all other addresses. Addresses of all new members are published in the Journal.

Please mail application and payment to the Canadian Numismatic Association, P.O. Box 226, Barrie, Ontario, Canada, L4M 4T2.

Application must be complete and accompanied by full dues to be accepted.

1976 MONTREAL OLYMPIC COINS

For the Summer Olympic Games of 1976, held in Montreal, seven series of silver coins were minted. There were four different coins in each series. Two $5.00 and two $10.00 coins, struck in sterling silver. The $5.00 coins weigh 24.4 grams and the $10.00 coins weigh 48.6 grams. The coins were available, encapsulated in plastic, as single coins, and in custom, prestige and proof four-coin sets. Each set of four coins, with a face value of $30.00, contains 4.28 oz. of fine silver. The purchase price of these sets is linked to the market price of silver, even if the intrinsic value falls below the face value. Large quantities of these coins were issued, and they are not redeemable by the government or the banks.

SERIES I

$5 Map of North America

$5 Kingston

$10 World Map

$10 Montreal

SERIES II

$5 Athlete with Torch

$5 Olive Wreath

41

$10 Head of Zeus

$10 Temple of Zeus

SERIES III

$5 Canoeing

$5 Rowing

$10 Lacrosse

$10 Bicycling

SERIES IV

$5 The Marathon

$5 Ladies' Javelin

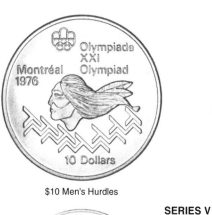

$10 Men's Hurdles

$10 Ladies Shot Put

SERIES V

$5 The Diver

$5 The Swimmer

$10 The Paddler

$10 Sailing

SERIES VI

$5 Fencing

$5 Boxing

43

$10 Field Hockey

$10 Football

SERIES VII

$5 Olympic Flame

$5 Olympic Village

$10 Olympic Stadium

$10 Olympic Velodrome

Date	Series	$5 Coin	$10 Coin	Custom Set	Prestige Set	Proof Set
1973	1	5.00	10.00	30.00	30.00	30.00
1974 Mule			100.00			
1974	2	5.00	10.00	30.00	30.00	30.00
1974	3	5.00	10.00	30.00	30.00	30.00
1975	4	5.00	10.00	30.00	30.00	30.00
1975	5	5.00	10.00	30.00	30.00	30.00
1976	6	5.00	10.00	30.00	30.00	32.00
1976	7	5.00	10.00	30.00	30.00	35.00

SILVER FIFTEEN DOLLAR COINS

OLYMPIC CENTENNIAL COINS

LUNAR CALENDER COINS

Common Obverse

1998 Obverse

Sports

1998 Year of the Tiger

Spirit

1999 Year of the Rabbit

ELIZABETH II 1992

Date	Description	Buying Price
1992	Sports	20.00
1992	Spirit	70.00

ELIZABETH II 1998-1999

Date	Description	Buying Price
1998	Tiger	35.00
1999	Rabbit	35.00

TWENTY DOLLAR COINS
1988 CALGARY OLYMPIC GAMES

The XV Winter Olympic Games were held in Calgary, February 13th to 29th, 1988. Ten different $20 silver coins were issued to commemorate this event. The coins weigh 34.107 grams, the composition is .925 silver and .075 copper, and they were issued in proof singles or proof sets in one or two coin display cases. Incorporated into the design of these coins are the letters "XV OLYMPIC WINTER GAMES - XVes JEUX OLYMPIQUE D'HIVER" impressed into the edge. During the striking of these coins at the Royal Canadian Mint, the impressed procedures were skipped on some series resulting in the edge lettering being missed on four known coins, resulting in varieties.

FIRST SERIES

Downhill Skiing

Speed Skating

SECOND SERIES

Hockey

Biathalon

THIRD SERIES

Cross-Country Skiing

Free-Style Skiing

FOURTH SERIES

Figure Skating

Curling

FIFTH SERIES

Ski Jumping

Bobsleigh

Date	Description	Buying Single	Buying Set
1985	Downhill Skiiing	20.00	
1985	Speed Skating	20.00	40.00
1985	Speed Skating, no edge lettering	100.00	
1986	Hockey	20.00	
1986	Hockey, no edge lettering	100.00	
1986	Biathalon	20.00	40.00
1986	Biathalon, no edge lettering	100.00	
1986	Cross-Country Skiing	20.00	
1986	Free-Style Skiing	20.00	40.00
1986	Free-Style Skiing, no edge lettering	100.00	
1987	Figure Skating	20.00	
1987	Curling	20.00	40.00
1987	Ski Jumping	20.00	
1987	Bobsleigh	20.00	40.00

TWENTY DOLLAR COINS

AVIATION
FIRST SERIES 1990 - 1994

Canada's aviation heroes and their achievements are commemorated on this first series of twenty dollar sterling-silver coins. The series is made up of ten coins, which were issued two per year over five years. For the first time, each coin design contains a 24-karat-gold -covered oval cameo portrait of the aviation hero commemorated. A maximum of 50,000 of each coin was offered for sale.

Coin No. 1
Anson and Harvard/Leckie

Coin No. 2
Lancaster/Fauquier

Coin No. 3 A.E.A. Silver Dart
F.W. Baldwin, John A. D.

Coin No. 4 de Havilland
Beaver/

Coin No. 5 Curtiss UN-4/
Sir F.W. Ballie

Coin No. 6 de Havilland
Gypsy Moth/ Murton A.

Coin No.7
Fairchild 71C/J.A.Richardson

Coin No. 8
Super Electra/Z.L.Leigh

Coin No. 9
Curtiss HS-2L/Stuart Graham

Coin No. 10
Vickers Vedette/T. Reid

Date	Description	Buying Price
1990	Anson and Harvard/Leckie	35.00
1990	Lancaster/Fauquier	100.00
1991	Silver Dart/Baldwin, McCurdy	30.00
1991	Beaver/Garratt	30.00
1992	Curtiss/Baille	30.00
1992	Gypsy Moth/Seymour	30.00
1993	Fairchild/Richardson	30.00
1993	Super Electra/Leigh	30.00
1994	Curtiss/Graham	30.00
1994	Vedette/Reid	30.00

AVIATION
SECOND SERIES 1995 - 1999

This second series of aviation coins celebrates "Powered Flight in Canada — Beyond World War II. As with the first series, it is made up of ten coins to be issued two per year over five years. Each coin design contains a 24-karat-gold-covered oval cameo portrait of the pilot, engineers or designers of the aircrafts. A maximum of 50,000 of each coin is offered for sale.

Coin No.1
The Fleet 80 Canuck/ Noury

Coin No. 2
DHC-1 Chipmunk/ Bannock

Coin No. 3
CF-100 Canuck/Zurakowski

Coin No. 4 CF-105
Arrow/Chamberlin

Date	Description	Buying Price
1995	Fleet 80 Canuck/Noury	35.00
1995	DHC-1 Chipmunk/Bannock	35.00
1996	CF-100 Canuck/Zurakowski	35.00
1996	CF-105 Arrow/Chamberlin	35.00

Coin No.5
F-86/Villeneuve

Coin No. 6
CT-11T/Tutor

Coin No. 7
CP-107 Argus/Longhurst

Coin No. 8
CL-218/Gagnon

Coin No. 9
Twin Otter/Neal

Coin No. 10
Dash 8/Fowler

Date	Description	Buying Price
1997	F-86/Villeneuve	35.00
1997	CT-11T/Tutor	35.00
1998	CP-107 Argus/Longhurst	35.00
1998	CL-215 Waterbomber/Gagnon	35.00
1999	Twin Otter/Neal	35.00
1999	Dash 8/Fowler	35.00

GOLD COINS

ONE HUNDRED DOLLARS

Canada issued the first one-hundred-dollar gold coin in 1976 to commemorate the Montreal Olympic Games. In that year two qualities and proportions of fineness were released; uncirculated coins were .585 fine (14 karat), and proof coins were .900 fine (22 karat). From 1976 to 1986, only proof quality coins with a fineness of .925 were issued. In 1987 the quality remained the same (proof), but the fineness of the coin was altered to .585 fine, or 14 karat, again.

IMPORTANT

Proof coins must be in mint-state condition. Mishandled, mounted or damaged coins are discounted from the prices listed. The buying price for gold coins is tied to the market price of gold. Any movement in the gold price will result in a corresponding price movement for these coins.

1976 - 14 kt   1976 - 22 kt

1977   1978   1979   1980

1981   1982   1983   1984

Date	Description	Fineness	Buying Price	Date	Description	Fineness	Buying Price
1976	14 kt Olympic	.585	105.00	1980	Arctic Territories	.916	190.00
1976	22 kt Olympic	.916	190.00	1981	"O Canada"	.916	190.00
1977	Jubilee	.916	190.00	1982	Constitution	.916	190.00
1978	Unity	.916	190.00	1983	Gilbert's Landing	.916	190.00
1979	Year of the Child	.916	190.00	1984	Voyage of Discovery	.916	190.00

ONE HUNDRED DOLLARS

1985	1986	1987	1988
1989	1990	1991	1992
1993	1994	1995	1996
1997	1998	1999	Photograph not available at press time
			2000

Date	Description	Fineness	Buying Price	Date	Description	Fineness	Buying Price
1985	National Parks	.916	190.00	1993	Horseless Carriage	.585	110.00
1986	Peace	.916	190.00	1994	The Home Front	.585	120.00
1987	Winter Olympic Games	.585	105.00	1995	Louisbourg	.585	120.00
1988	Bowhead Whale	.585	105.00	1996	Klondike Gold Rush	.585	140.00
1989	Ste. Marie	.585	105.00	1997	Alexander Graham Bell	.585	150.00
1990	Literacy Year	.585	105.00	1998	Insulin	.585	175.00
1991	Empress of India	.585	105.00	1999	Newfoundland	.585	175.00
1992	Montreal	.585	110.00	2000	N/A	.585	175.00

TWO HUNDRED DOLLARS

1990	1991	1992	1993	

1994	1995	1996	1997	

Photograph not availablae at press time	Photograph not available at press time

1998	1999	2000	2001

Date	Description	Fineness	Buying Price	Date	Description	Fineness	Buying Price
1990	Canada Flag	.916	200.00	1996	Transcontinental	.916	250.00
1991	A National Passion	.916	200.00	1997	Haida	.916	275.00
1992	Niagara Falls	.916	210.00	1998	White Buffalo	.916	275.00
1993	RCMP	.916	210.00	1999	Butterfly	.916	275.00
1994	Anne of Green Gables	.916	210.00	2000	N/A	—	—
1995	Sugar Bush	.916	225.00	2001	N/A	—	—

175 AND 350 DOLLAR GOLD COINS

175 DOLLAR GOLD COIN

350 DOLLAR GOLD COINS

ELIZABETH II 1992

Date	Description	Buying Price
1992	Olympic	200.00

1999
Photograph
not
available
at press
time

ELIZABETH II 1998-1999

Date	Description	Buying Price
1998	90th Anniversary	450.00
1999	Lady's Slipper	450.00

PROOF PLATINUM COINS

In 1990 the Royal Canadian Mint entered the luxury market for high-quality collector coins. The platinum coin sets are comprised of four coins all depicting some facet of the life of the animal in its natural habitat. The coin denominations in the sets are $300, $150, $75 and $30.

1990 Polar Bears	1991 Snowy Owls	1992 Cougars
1993 Arctic Foxes	1994 Otters	1995 Lynx
1996 Peregrine Falcons	1997 Wood Bisons	1998 Wolves

Date	Description	Buying Price	Date	Description	Buying Price
1990	Polar Bear Set	1,000.00	1996	Falcon $150	325.00
1991	Snowy Owl Set	1,000.00	1997	Bison Set	1,500.00
1992	Cougar Set	1,100.00	1997	Bison $30	65.00
1993	Arctic Fox Set	1,100.00	1997	Bison $150	325.00
1994	Otter Set	1,100.00	1998	Wolf Set	1,500.00
1995	Lynx Set	1,250.00	1998	Wolf $30	65.00
1995	Lynx $30	65.00	1998	Wolf $150	325.00
1995	Lynx $150	325.00	1999	Muskox $35.00	65.00
1996	Falcon Set	1,250.00	1999	Muskox Set	1500.00
1996	Falcon $30	65.00			

Note: 1999 Illustrations not available at press time

MAPLE LEAF BULLION COINS

The Maple Leaf gold coins were first produced in 1979, the fractional or small sizes three years later in 1982, and the half-ounce size in 1986. In 1988 the four sizes; $5.00, $10.00, $20.00 and $50.00, of platinum were added. Expanding the range in 1993, $1.00 gold and platinum coins were issued, and again in 1994 $2.00 coins were placed on the market.

The price of Maple Leaf bullion coins is based on the spot market on the day of purchase, times their gold content, less a small handling charge.

$50 $20 $10 $5

COIN SPECIFICATIONS

Denomination	Description	Content	Weight Tr. Oz.
$1	1/20 Maple	Gold or platinum	.050
$2	1/15 Maple	Gold or platinum	.667
$5	1/10 Maple	Gold or platinum	.100
$10	1/4 Maple	Gold or platinum	.250
$20	1/2 Maple	Gold or platinum	.500
$50	Maple	Gold or platinum	1.00
$5	Maple	Silver	1.00
$50	10 Maple	Silver	10.00

MAPLE LEAF PROOF BULLION ISSUES OF 1989

To commemorate the tenth anniversary of the Maple Leaf bullion program, the Royal Canadian Mint, in 1989, issued a series of proof condition silver, gold and platinum coins, individually and in sets. The single coins and sets were packaged in solid maple presentation cases with brown velvet liners.

Type	Description	Buying Price
Sets	Gold 4 coins: 1, 1/2, 1/4, 1/10 ounce maple	800.00
	Platinum 4 coins: 1, 1/2, 1/4, 1/4, 1/10 ounce maple	1,000.00
	Gold and Platinum 1/10 ounce maple each, Silver 1 ounce Maple, 3 coins	115.00
	Gold, Platinum and Silver 3 coins: 1 ounce maple each	1,100.00
Singles	Gold, One Maple	450.00
	Silver, One Maple	20.00

COLLECTOR SETS

SILVER PROOF-LIKE SETS

Date	Description	Buying Price
1954	Voyageur	160.00
1955	Voyageur	110.00
1955	Arnprior	135.00
1956	Voyageur	65.00
1957	Voyageur	35.00
1958	British Columbia	30.00
1959	Voyageur	15.00
1960	Voyageur	78.00
1961	Voyageur	78.00
1962	Voyageur	7.00
1963	Voyageur	7.00
1964	Charlottetown	7.00
1965	Voyageur	7.00
1966	Voyageur	7.00
1967	Centennial	8.00

NICKEL PROOF-LIKE SETS

Date	Description	Buying Price
1968	Voyageur	2.00
1969	Voyageur	2.00
1970	Manitoba	2.00
1971	British Columbia	2.00
1972	Voyageur	2.00
1973	R.C.M.P., Small Bust	2.00
1973	R.C.M.P., Large Bust	75.00
1974	Winnipeg	2.00
1975	Voyageur	2.00
1976	Voyageur	2.00
1977	Voyageur	2.00
1978	Voyageur	2.00
1979	Voyageur	2.00
1980	Voyageur	3.00
1981	Voyageur	2.00

NICKEL PROOF-LIKE SETS

Date	Description	Buying Price
1982	Voyageur	2.00
1983	Voyageur	3.00
1984	Voyageur	3.00
1985	Voyageur	3.00
1986	Voyageur	4.00
1987	Voyageur	3.00
1988	Loon	3.00
1989	Loon	5.00
1990	Loon	5.00
1991	Loon	15.00
1992	Loon	8.00
1993	Loon	4.00
1994	Loon	4.00
1994	"O Canada"	5.00
1995	Loon	4.00
1995	"O Canada"	5.00
1995	"Baby Set"	6.00
1996	Loon/Polar Bear	10.00
1996	"O Canada"	9.00
1996	"Baby Set"	9.00
1997	Loon/Polar Bear	6.00
1997	"O Canada"	8.00
1997	"Baby Set"	8.00
1998W	Loon/Polar Bear	15.00
1998	Loon/Polar Bear	8.00
1998W	"O Canada"	10.00
1998W	"Baby Set"	10.00
1999	Loon/Polar Bear	4.00
1999	"O Canada"	8.00
1999	"Baby Set"	8.00
2000	Loon/Polar Bear	
2000	"O Canada"	
2000	"Baby Set"	

Note: Sets with the Mint mark "W" were struck in Winnipeg

SPECIMEN SETS

Issued by the Royal Canadian Mint starting in 1981 and continuing to date, contains one cent to the nickel dollar (six coins).

Date	Description	Buying Price
1981	Voyageur	3.00
1982	Voyageur	3.00
1983	Voyageur	3.50
1984	Voyageur	3.50
1985	Voyageur	3.50
1986	Voyageur	3.50
1987	Voyageur	3.50
1988	Loon	4.00
1989	Loon	6.00
1990	Loon	6.00
1991	Loon	15.00
1992	Loon	9.00
1993	Loon	6.00
1994	Loon	8.00
1995	Loon	8.00
1996	Loon/Polar Bear	10.00
1997	Flying loon	10.00
1998	Loon/Polar Bear	10.00
1999	Loon/Polar Bear	10.00
2000	Loon/Polar Bear	10.00

PRESTIGE PROOF SETS

Issued by the Royal Canadian Mint in 1971 and continuing to date, these sets contain one cent to the nickel dollar plus the silver dollar (listed below), a total of seven coins.

Date	Description	Buying Price
1971	British Columbia	8.00
1972	Voyageur	10.00
1973	R.C.M.P., Small Bust	8.00
1973	R.C.M.P., Large Bust	75.00
1974	Winnipeg	8.00
1975	Calgary	8.00
1976	Parliament	8.00
1977	Jubilee	8.00
1978	Commonwealth Games	8.00
1979	Griffon	10.00
1980	Arctic Territories	18.00
1981	Trans Canada	14.00
1982	Regina	9.00
1983	University Games	9.00
1984	Toronto	9.00
1985	National Parks	9.00
1986	Vancouver	9.00
1987	Davis Straits	10.00
1988	Ironworks	18.00
1989	MacKenzie River	18.00
1990	Henry Kelsey	18.00
1991	Frontenac	35.00

Date	Description	Buying Price
1992	Stagecoach	25.00
1993	Hockey	15.00
1994	RCMP	20.00
1994	RCMP Red Box	20.00
1995	Hudson's Bay	30.00
1995	Hudson's Bay Red Box	25.00
1996	John McIntosh	35.00
1997	Canada/Russia Hockey	40.00
1998	RCMP 125th Anniversary	40.00
1999	Juan Perez	40.00
2000	N/A	40.00

CUSTOM SETS

These sets were issued by the Royal Canadian Mint between 1971 and 1980. They contain seven coins, the one cent to the nickel dollar, plus an extra cent.

Date	Description	Buying Price
1971 to 1980		2.00

PROOF SETS

Sets of specimen coins have been issued in Canada at various times since 1858, often in official cases. A representative selection follows. Sets from 1908 are in leather or leatherette-covered presentation cases.

Date	Description	Buying Price
1858	Victoria: 1, 5, 10, 20 cents	3,000.00
1870	Victoria: 5, 10, 25, 50 cents	8,000.00
1908	Edward VII: 1, 5, 10, 25, 50 cents	1,000.00
1911	George V: 1, 5, 10, 25, 50 cents	3,000.00
1937	George VI: 1, 5, 10, 25, 50 cents $1	500.00
1937	George VI: as above, but in card case	250.00
1967	Elizabeth II: Centennial, 1, 5, 10, 25, 50 cents $1.00, $20.00 gold	200.00
1967	Elizabeth II: Centennial, as above, but with medal instead of $20.00 gold	10.00
1998	Elizabeth II: Reissued 1908-1998	
	Matte	50.00
	Proof	50.00

PAPER MONEY OF CANADA

PROVINCE OF CANADA

1866 ISSUES

Denom.	Issue Date	Buying Price	Denom.	Issue Date	Buying Price
$1	1866	400.00	$10	1866	2,000.00
$2	1866	1,000.00	$20	1866	3,000.00
$5	1866	1,500.00	$50	1866	5,500.00

DOMINION OF CANADA

1870 ISSUES

Plain   Series Letter A   Series Letter B

Denom.	Issue Date	Buying Price	Denom.	Issue Date	Buying Price
25-cent Plain	1870	10.00	25-cent Series B	1870	12.00
25-cent Series A	1870	50.00			

Note: Buying prices are for notes in VG condition

1870 ISSUES

Denom.	Issue Date	Variety/Signature	Buying Price
$1	1870	Payable at Montreal or Toronto	225.00
$1	1870	Payable at Halifax	375.00
$1	1870	Payable at St. John	375.00
$2	1870	Payable at Montreal or Toronto	1,200.00
$2	1870	Payable at Halifax or St. John	2,200.00

1878 ISSUES

Denom.	Issue Date	Variety/Signature	Buying Price
$1	1878	Scalloped Frame, Payable at Montreal or Toronto	200.00
$1	1878	Scalloped Frame, Payable at St. John or Halifax	550.00
$1	1878	Lettered Frame, Payable at Montreal or Toronto	60.00
$1	1878	Lettered Frame, Payable at St. John or Halifax	350.00
$2	1878	Payable at Montreal or Toronto	600.00
$2	1878	Payable at St. John or Halifax	1,200.00

1882 AND 1887 ISSUES

Denom.	Issue Date	Variety/Signature	Buying Price
$4	1882		600.00
$2	1887	Plain, Series A	250.00

1897 AND 1898 ISSUES

| No "One" | Inward "One" | Outward "One" |

Denom.	Issue Date	Variety/Signature	Buying Price
$1	1897	Green face tint	150.00
$2	1897	Red-brown back	300.00
$2	1897	Dark brown back	75.00
$1	1898	Inward "One"	50.00
$1	1898	Outward "One"	30.00

1900 AND 1902 ISSUES

| "4" on Top | "Four" on Top |

Denom.	Issue Date	Variety/Signature	Buying Price
25-cent	1900	Courtney	2.00
25-cent	1900	Bouville	2.00
25-cent	1900	Saunders	2.00
$4	1900		325.00
$4	1902	"4" on Top	325.00
$4	1902	"Four" on Top	325.00

Note: All buying prices are for notes in very good condition.

1911 AND 1912 ISSUES

| No Seal | Seal over Five | Seal Only |

Denom.	Issue Date	Variety/Signature	Buying Price
$1	1911	Green Line or Black Line	25.00
$500	1911		3,250.00
$1,000	1911		3,750.00
$5	1912	No Seal	150.00
$5	1912	Seal over Five	150.00
$5	1912	Seal Only	150.00

1914 AND 1917 ISSUES

Denom.	Issue Date	Variety/Signature	Buying Price
$2	1914	No Seal	40.00
$2	1914	Seal over Two	95.00
$2	1914	Seal Only	50.00
$1	1917	No Seal	22.50
$1	1917	Seal over One	27.50
$1	1917	Black Seal	22.50

1923 ISSUES

Denom.	Issue Date	Variety/Signature	Buying Price
25-cent	1923	Hyndman/Saunders	2.00
25-cent	1923	McCavour/Saunders	2.00
25-cent	1923	Campbell/Clark	2.00
$1	1923	Various Colour Seals	17.50
$1	1923	Purple Seal	37.50
$2	1923	Various Colours Seals	27.50
$2	1923	Green Seal	25.00
$2	1923	Bronze Seal	25.00

1924 AND 1925 ISSUES

Denom.	Issue Date	Variety/Signature	Buying Price
$5	1924	Queen Mary	825.00
$500	1925	George V	4,500.00
$1,000	1925	Queen Mary	5,500.00

Note: All buying prices are for notes in very good condition.

1935 ISSUES

Denom.	Variety	Buying Price
$1	English text	10.00
$1	French text	10.00
$2	English text	15.00
$2	French text	25.00
$5	English text	27.50
$5	French text	35.00
$10	English text	27.50
$10	French text	35.00
$20	English text, small seal	60.00
$20	English text, large seal	85.00

Denom.	Variety	Buying Price
$20	French text	125.00
$25	English text	350.00
$25	French text	450.00
$50	English text	225.00
$50	French text	275.00
$100	English text	125.00
$100	French text	200.00
$500	English or French	5,500.00
$1,000	English or French	1,050.00

1937 ISSUES

IMPORTANT

Bank notes with tears, missing corners, pinholes or folding creases are not considered to be very fine (VF). Notes in poor condition are not collectable.

Denom.	Very Fine Buying Prices By Signature		
	Osborne	Gordon	Coyne
$1	5.00	3.00	3.00
$2	7.00	5.00	5.00
$5	20.00	6.00	6.00
$10	14.00	10.00	10.00
$20	25.00	20.00	20.00
$50	100.00	50.00	50.00
$100	110.00	100.00	100.00
$1,000	1,025.00	Not Issued	

1954 ISSUES

"DEVIL'S FACE" PORTRAIT

IMPORTANT

The buying prices listed below are for notes in extremely fine condition. The notes must be clean with no tears, pinholes or noticeable folds or creases.

THE DEVIL'S FACE NOTES

On the earliest notes of the 1954 issue, highlighted areas of the Queen's hair produced the illusion of a leering demonic face behind her ear. This was not the result of an error, nor was it, as some have asserted, the prank of an IRA sympathizer at the bank note company. It was merely the faithful reproduction of the original photograph. The portrait of the Queen with the devil's face outlined in her hair generated almost instant controversy.

ASTERISK NOTES

Asterisk notes are replacement notes, the first being spoiled in printing, cutting, etc., and replaced by an asterisk note.

	Very Fine Buying Price by Signature			
	Coyne/Towers		Beattie/Coyne	
Denom.	Regular	Asterisk	Regular	Asterisk
$1	3.00	75.00	2.00	50.00
$2	3.50	150.00	3.00	100.00
$5	7.00	300.00	7.00	150.00
$10	11.00	250.00	11.00	125.00
$20	22.00	250.00	20.00	200.00
$50	50.00	NI	50.00	NI
$100	100.00	NI	100.00	NI
$1,000	1,000.00	NI	NI	NI

*NI - Not Issued

MODIFIED PORTRAIT

IMPORTANT

The buying prices listed below are for notes in uncirculated condition (new). The note must be clean, crisp, with no tears, creases, folds or marks of any kind or description.

MODIFIED PORTRAIT

The portrait was modified by darkening the highlights in the hair and thus removing the shading which had resulted in the devil's face. The modification of the face plates was made for most denominations in 1956, except for the $1,000 denomination, which was modified several years later.

	Uncirculated Buying Price by Signature							
	Beattie/Coyne		Beattie/Rasminsky		Bouey/Raminsky		Lawson/Bouey	
Denom.	Regular	Astrisk	Regular	Asterisk	Regular	Asterisk	Regular	Asterisk
$1	1.75	10.00	1.75	3.00	1.75	3.00	1.75	2.00
$2	6.00	20.00	2.50	4.00	2.50	3.00	2.50	4.00
$5	10.00	20.00	7.50	10.00	10.00	15.00	NI	NI
$10	15.00	25.00	12.50	15.00	NI	NI	NI	NI
$20	30.00	40.00	25.00	40.00	NI	NI	NI	NI
$50	60.00	NI	55.00	NI	NI	NI	100.00	NI
$100	105.00	NI	105.00	NI	NI	NI	105.00	NI
$1,000	1,000.00	NI	1,000.00	NI	1,000.00	NI	1,000.00	NI

*NI - Not Issued

$1 CENTENNIAL 1967

For the centennial of Canada's Confederation a special $1 note was issued. The note has a single design and two types of serial numbers, regular serial numbers and a special number "1867 - 1967." The special series was available from the Bank of Canada as a collector's item, but examples were soon found in circulation. In addition, there was an asterisk note series for replacement notes.

Denom.	Issue Date	Variety	Uncirculated Buying Price
$1	1967	Commemorative Serial Number 1867-1967	1.10
$1	1967	Regular Serial Number	1.10
$1	1967	Asterisk Serial Number	2.00

1969 - 1975 ISSUE

This new series combined fine line engraving with subtle variations to make notes that are extremely difficult to counterfeit. The series features a new portrait of the Queen, as well as portraits of previous prime ministers of Canada.

IMPORTANT

The buying prices listed on the following page are for notes in uncirculated condition (new). The note must be clean, crisp, with no tears, creases, folds or marks of any kind or description.

ASTERISK AND "X" REPLACEMENT NOTES

Replacement of defective notes by asterisk notes was continued when the 1968-1975 issue was introduced. The highest denomination of the 1954 issue to be printed with asterisks was the $20; however, all denominations in the 1969-1975 issue, including the $50 and $100 notes, occur with asterisks in front of the two-letter prefix type.

When the triple-letter prefix notes were introduced in 1981, the use of the asterisk was discontinued. For triple-letter prefix notes, a replacement note was then designated by the use of an "X" for the third letter.

Asterisk Notes	"X" Replacement Notes
BC-46aA	BC-46A-i

	Uncirculated Buying Price by Signature							
	Beattie/Rasminsky		Bouey/Rasminsky		Lawson/Bouey		Crow/Bouey	
Denom.	Regular	Asterisk	Regular	Asterisk	Regular	Asterisk	Regular	Asterisk
$1	NI	NI	NI	NI	1.25	1.50	1.00	1.50
$2	NI	NI	NI	NI	2.25	4.00	2.00	20.00
$5	NI	NI	7.50	10.00	7.00	8.00	NI	NI
$10	15.00	20.00	20.00	15.00	12.00	15.00	12.00	15.00
$20	22.00	25.00	NI	NI	22.00	25.00	NI	NI
$50	NI	NI	NI	NI	50.00	60.00	50.00	55.00
$100	NI	NI	NI	NI	100.00	105.00	100.00	105.00

Note: The Thiessen/Crow combination of signatures does not command a numismatic premium at this time.

*NI - Not Issued

1979 ISSUES

The series beginning in 1979 is a modification of the previous issue. The face designs are similar, as is the colouration. The serial numbers are moved to the back of the note at the bottom, where the name of the Bank of Canada previously appeared. The black serial numbers are machine readable.

IMPORTANT

The buying prices listed below are for notes in uncirculated condition (new). The note must be clean, crisp, with no tears, creases, folds or marks of any kind or description.

REPLACEMENT NOTES

There are no asterisk notes in this issue. The replacement notes are designated by the second digit in the serial number.

The digit 1 following the first digit 3 of the $5 notes designates a replacement note. In the $20 denomination the replacement notes can be distinguished by "510" for the CBN company and "516" for the BABN company.

$5 Replacement Note $20 Replacement Note

| Denom. | Uncirculated Buying Price by Signature | | | | | |
| | Lawson/Bouey | | Crow/Bouey | | Thiessen/Crow | |
	Regular	Asterisk	Regular	Astrisk	Reguar	Asterisk
$5	7.50	30.00	7.50	60.00	NI	NI
$20	25.00	30.00	20.00	25.00	20.00	25.00

1986 ISSUES

On March 14, 1986, the Bank of Canada introduced a new series of bank notes. The new designs were launched that year with the issue of the $2 and $5 notes. The $1 and $2 bank notes have been replaced with $1 and $2 coins.

$5 Replacement Note

| Denom. | Uncirculated Buying Price by Signature | | | | | |
| | Crow/Bouey | | Thiessen/Crow | | Bonin/Thiessen | |
	Regular	Asterick	Regular	Asterick	Regular	Asterick
$2	4.00	8.00	3.00	5.00	2.00	10.00
$5	8.00	20.00	5.00	8.00	5.00	15.00
$10	N/I	N/I	11.00	15.00	10.00	15.00
$20	N/I	N/I	21.00	25.00	20.00	25.00
$50	N/I	N/I	55.00	60.00	50.00	N/I
$100	N/I	N/I	100.00	110.00	100.00	N/I
$1000	N/I	N/I	1,000.00	1,200.00	1,000.00	N/I

NEWFOUNDLAND
PUBLIC WORKS CASH NOTES

1901-1909

Denom.	Buying Price
40 cents	70.00
50 cents	70.00
80 cents	70.00
$1	90.00
$5	425.00

1910-1911

Denom.	Buying Price
25 cents	25.00
50 cents	25.00
$1	40.00
$2	350.00
$5	450.00

GOVERNMENT NOTES

Denom.	Buying Price
$1	30.00
$2	60.00

PRINCE EDWARD ISLAND

Denom.	Buying Price
1848-1870 £1	275.00
1872 $10	225.00
1872 $20	225.00

NOVA SCOTIA

Denom.	Buying Price
1848-1854 £1	85.00
1861 $5	175.00

CANADIAN NOTE-ISSUING BANKS

The following list of banks identifies in alphabetical order all the non-government banks which issued or ordered Canadian notes.

Bank notes were first issued in Canada in 1813 and continued until 1943. One hundred and sixty different banks issued notes and some over a long period of time. There are literally thousands of different notes and if you add different grades, the number rises to tens of thousands. Far beyond the scope of this guide.

If you have a bank note that is on this list of banks then it is Canadian and please check with your local dealer for current buying prices.

The Bank of Acadia, Liverpool, N.S., 1872-1873
The Accommodation Bank, Kingston, U.C., 1836-1837
The Agricultural Bank, Montreal, L.C., 1837
The Agricultural Bank, Toronto, U.C., 1834-1837
Arman's Bank, Montreal, L.C., 1837
Barclay's Bank (Canada), Montreal, Que., 1929-1956
La Banque du Boucherville, Boucherville, L.C., 1830's
The Bank of Brantford, Brantford, C.W., 1857-1860's
The British Canadian Bank, Toronto, Ont., 1883-1884
The Bank of British Columbia, Victoria, B.C., 1862-1901
The Bank of British North America, 1836-1918
Canada Bank, Montreal, L.C., 1792
The Canada Bank, Toronto, C.W., 1855
The Bank of Canada, Montreal, L.C., 1813-1831
The Canadian Bank of Commerce, Toronto, Ont., 1867-1961
Banque Canadienne, St. Hyacinthe, L.C., 1836-1838
Banque Canadienne Nationale, Montreal, Que., 1924-1979
The Central Bank of Canada, Toronto, Ont., 1883-1887
Central Bank of New Brunswick, Fredericton, N.B., 1834-1866
Charlotte County Bank, St. Andrew's, N.B., 1825-1865
Bank of Charlottetown, Charlottetown, P.E.I., 1852
The City Bank, Montreal, L.C., 1833-1876
City Bank, Saint John, N.B., 1836-1839
The Bank of Clifton, C.W., 1859-1863
The Colonial Bank of Canada, Toronto, C.W., 1856-1863
The Colonial Bank of Chatham, Chatham, U.C., 1837-1839
Commerical Bank, Brockville, U.C., 1837
Commercial Bank, Kingston, U.C., 1837
The Commercial Bank of Canada, Kingston, C.W., 1856-1868
The Commercial Bank of Fort Erie, Fort Erie, U.C., 1836-1839
The Commercial Bank of Lake Ontario, Niagara Falls, U.C., 1837
The Commercial Bank of Manitoba, Winnipeg, Man., 1885-1893
The Commerical Bank of the Midland District, Kingston, U.C., 1831-1856
Commerical Bank of Montreal, Montreal, L.C., 1835-1837
Commercial Bank of New Brunswick, Saint John, N.B., 1834-1868
The Commercial Bank of Newfoundland, St. John's, Nfld., 1857-1894
Commercial Bank of Windsor, Windsor, N.S., 1864-1902
Commerical Branch Bank of Canada, Collingwood, C.W., 1861-1879
The Consolidated Bank of Canada, Montreal, Que., 1876-1879
The Bank of the County of Elgin, St. Thomas, C.W., 1857-1862
The Crown Bank of Canada, Toronto, Ont., 1904-1908
The Dominion Bank, Toronto, Ont., 1869-1955
Eastern Bank of Canada, Saint John, N.B., 1928-1934
The Eastern Townships Bank, Sherbrooke, C.E., 1855-1912
The Exchange Bank, Quebec, L.C., 1840's
The Exchange Bank of Canada, Montreal, Que., 1871-1883
The Exchange Bank of Canada, Windsor, Ont., 1860's

The Exchange Bank of Toronto, C.W., 1855
The Exchange Bank of Yarmouth, Yarmouth, N.S., 1867-1903
The Exchange Bank Company of Chippewa, Chippewa, U.C., 1837
The Farmer's Bank, Toronto, U.C., 1840's
The Farmers Bank of Canada, Toronto, Ont., 1906-1910
The Farmer's Bank of Malden, Maiden, U.C., 1840's
The Farmer's Joint Stock Banking Co., Toronto, U.C., 1835-1849
The Farmers J.S. Banking Co., Toronto, U.C., 1830's
The Farmers Bank of Rustico, Rustico, P.E.I., 1862-1892
The Farmers Bank of St. John's, St. John's, L.C., 1837-1838
The Federal Bank of Canada, Toronto, Ont., 1874-1888
The Bank of Fredericton, Fredericton, N.B., 1836-1839
The Free Holders Bank of the Midland District, Bath, U.C., 1837
Goderich Bank, Goderich, U.C., 1834
The Gore Bank, Hamilton, U.C., 1835-1870
The Gore Bank of Hamilton, Hamilton, U.C., c.1837
The Grenville County Bank, Prescott, C.W., 1856
The Halifax Banking Company, Halifax, N.S., 1825-1903
The Hamtilon Bank, Hamilton, L.C., 1835
The Bank of Hamilton, Hamilton, Ont., 1872-1923
Hart's Bank, Three Rivers, L.C., 1835-1847
Henry's Bank, La Prairie and Montreal, L.C., 1837
Banque d'Hochelaga, Montreal, Que., 1873-1925
The Home Bank of Canada, Toronto, Ont., 1903-1923
The Bank of Hull, Hull, L.C., 1837
The Imperial Bank of Canada, Toronto, Ont., 1873-1961
The International Bank of Canada, Toronto, U.C., 1858-1859
Banque Internationale du Canada, Montreal, Que., 1911-1913
La Banque Jacques Cartier, Montreal, C.E., 1861-1900
The Kingston Bank, Kingston, L.C., 1837
The Bank of Liverpool, Liverpool, N.S., 1871-1879
The Bank of London in Canada, London, Ont., 1883-1888
Lower Canada Bank, Montreal, L.C., 1837
The Bank of Lower Canada, Quebec, L.C., late 1830's MacDonald & Co., Victoria, B.C.,
     1859-1866
The Maritime Bank of the Dominon of Canada, Saint John, N.B., 1872-1887
The Mechanics Bank, Montreal, L.C., 1837
The Mechanics Bank, Montreal, C.E., 1865-1879
The Mechanics Bank of Saint John's, Saint John's, L.C., 1837
The Mercantile Banking Corporation, Halifax, N.S., 1878
The Merchants Bank, Montreal, C.E., 1864-1868
The Merchants Bank, Toronto, U.C., 1837
The Merchants Bank of Canada, Montreal, Que., 1868-1923
The Merchants Bank of Halifax, Halifax, N.S., 1864-1901
The Merchants Bank of Prince Edward Island, Charlottetown, P.E.I., 1871-1906
The Merchants Exchange Bank, Goderich, C.W., 1853
The Metropolitan Bank, Montreal, Que., 1871-1876
The Metropolitan Bank, Toronto, 1902-1914
The Molsons Bank, Montreal, C.E., 1837-1925
Montreal Bank, Montreal, L.C., 1817-1822
The Montreal Bank, Montreal, C.W., 1840's-1950's
The Bank of Montreal, Montreal, L.C., 1822 to date
La Banque Nationale, Montreal, C.E., 1860-1925
The Bank of New Brunswick, Saint John, N.B., 1820-1913
The Newcastle Banking Co., Amherst, U.C., 1836
The Newcastle District Loan Company, Peterborough, U.C., 1836
The Newcastle District Bank, St. Catharines, C.W., 1853-1875
The Niagara Suspension Bridge Bank, Queenston, U.C., 1836-1841
The Northern Bank, Winnpeg, Man., 1905-1908

The Northern Crown Bank, Winnipeg, Man., 1908-1918
The Bank of Nova Scotia, Halifax, N.S., 1832 to date
The Ontario Bank, Bowmanville, C.W., 1857-1906
The Bank of Ottawa, Montreal, L.C., 1837
The Bank of Ottawa, Ont., 1874-1919
The Bank of the People, Toronto, U.C., 1835-1841
La Banque du Peuple, Montreal, L.C., 1835-1895
The People's Bank of Halifax, Halifax, N.S., 1864-1905
The People's Bank of New Brunswick, Fredericton, N.B., 1864-1907
The Phenix Bank, Phillipsburg, L.C., 1837-1841
The Pictou Bank, Pictou, N.S., 1873-1887
The Bank of Prince Edward Island, Charlottetonwn, P.E.I., 1856-1881
The Provincial Bank, London, Ont., 1884
The Provincial Bank of Canada, Stanstead, Ont., 1856-1863
La Banque Provinciale du Canada, Montreal, Que., 1900-1979
The Quebec Bank, Quebec, L.C., 1818-1917
Bank of Quebec Lower Canada, Quebec, L.C., 1841
The Royal Bank of Canada, Montreal, Que., 1901 to date
The Royal Canadian Bank, Toronto, C.W., 1864-1876
The Saint Francis Bank, Stanstead, C.E., 1855
La Banque de St. Hyacinthe St. Hyacinthe, Que., 1873-1908
La Banque de St. Jean, St. Jean, Que., 1873-1908
Banque St. Jean Baptiste, Montreal, Que., 1875
The St. Lawrence Bank, Toronto, Ont., 1872-1876
The St. Lawrence Bank & Lumber Co., Malbaie, L.C., 1837
The St. Stephen's Bank, St. Stephen, N.B., 1836-1910
The Bank of Saskatchewan, Moose Jaw, Sask., 1913
The Sovereign Bank of Canada, Montreal, Que., 1901-1908
The Stadacona Bank, Quebec City, Que., 1872-1879
The Standard Bank of Canada, Toronto,Ont., 1876-1928
The Sterling Bank of Canada, Toronto, Ont., 1905-1924
The Summerside Bank, Summerside, P.E.I., 1866-1901
Tattersall Bank, Montreal, L.C., 183-
The Bank of Toronto, Toronto, Ont., 1855-1954
The Traders Bank of Canada, Toronto, Ont., 1885-1912
The Union Bank, Montreal, L.C., 1838-c.1840
The Union Bank of Canada, Quebec City, Que., 1886-1925
THe Union Bank of Halifax, Halifax, N.S., 1856-1910
The Union Bank of Lower Canada, Quebec, C.E., 1865-1886
The Union Bank of Montreal, Montreal, L.C., c.1840
Union Bank of Newfoundland, St. John's, Nfld., 1854-1894
The Union Bank of Prince Edward Island, Charlottetown, P.E.I., 1860-1893
Unite Empire Bank of Canada, Toronto,Ont., 1906-1911
Bank of Upper Canada, Kingston, U.C., 1819-1822
Bank of Upper Canada, York, U.C., 1821-1866
The Bank of Vancouver, Vancouver, B.C., 1910-1914
The Bank of Victoria, Victoria, U.C., 1836
La Banque Ville Marie, Montreal, Que., 1872-1899
The Bank of Western Canada, Clifton, C.W., 1859-1863
The Western Bank of Canada, Oshawa, Ont., 1882-1909
The Westmoreland Bank of New Brunswick, N.B., 1854-1867
The Weyburn Security Bank, Weyburn, Sask., 1910-1931
The Bank of Yarmouth, Yarmouth, N.S., 1859-1905
The Zimmerman Bank, Elgin., C.W., 1854-1859

COLONIAL COINS AND TOKENS

Canada has produced a great number of tokens of various kinds over the years. Tokens were used as a form of currency prior to the institution of the decimal currency system in 1858 (Colonial issues are not all tokens, some being regal coins). After Confederation, other kinds of tokens appeared, such as those for services, transportation and advertising purposes.

The prices in this section are for tokens in VG (very good) or F (fine) condition. Higher prices will be paid for rare issues or for tokens in VF (very fine) or better condition.

NEWFOUNDLAND TOKENS

Date and Description	Buying Price	Date and Description	Buying Price
Rutherford - St. John's	2.50	1858 Sailing Ship	80.00
Rutherford - Harbour Grace	2.50	1860 Fishery Rights	12.00
McAuslane	1,000.00		

PRINCE EDWARD ISLAND TOKENS

Date and Description	Buying Price	Date and Description	Buying Price
Holey Dollar Ring*	1,200.00	McCarthy Penny	600.00
Holey Dollar Plug*	1,200.00	Sheaf of Wheat	150.00
McCausland Penny	600.00	Speed The Plough	1.50

Note: Forgeries exist and are worth considerably less.

PRINCE EDWARD ISLAND TOKENS

Date and Description	Buying Price	Date and Description	Buying Price
Fisheries & Agriculture	2.00	Fisheries & Agriculture	2.00
Self Government 1855 Prince Edward's	2.00	Ships Colonies 1815 One Penny	6.00
Self Government 1855 Prince Edward	2.00	Ships Colonies 1815 Publick Accommodation	6.00
Self Government 1857	2.00	Ships Colonies	2.00

Note: Tokens must be VG (very good) or better, with no discolouration.

NOVA SCOTIA
SEMI-REGAL TOKENS

Date and Description	Buying Price	Date and Description	Buying Price
1823 Halfpenny	.50	1840 Halfpenny	.50
1823 Penny	1.00	1840 Penny	1.00
1824 Halfpenny	.50	1843 Half Penny	.50
1824 Penny	1.00	1843 Penny	1.00
1832 Halfpenny	.50	1856 Halfpenny	.50
1832 Penny	1.00	1856 Penny	1.00

NOVA SCOTIA
PRIVATE TOKENS

Date and Description	Buying Price	Date and Description	Buying Price
Broke - Halifax	2.00	Hosterman & Etter 1815	2.00
Convenience of Trade	3.00	Starr & Shannon	1.00
Carritt & Alport	3.00	Commercial Change	1.00
Hosterman & Etter	2.00	Miles W. White	1.00

NOVA SCOTIA
PRIVATE TOKENS

Date and Description	Buying Price	Date and Description	Buying Price
John Alexr Barry	1.00	Trade & Navigation 1812	1.00
Halifax Nova Scotia	2.00	Trade & Navigation 1813	15.00
W. A. & S. Black's	2.00	Pure Copper Preferable	1.00
J. Brown	1.00	Success to Navigation	1.00
W. L. White's	15.00	N.S & N.B. Success	15.00

NEW BRUNSWICK TOKENS

Date and Description	Buying Price	Date and Description	Buying Price
1843 Halfpenny	.50	McDermott	250.00
1843 Penny	.75	St. John	2.00
1854 Halfpenny	.50	St. John's	1,500.00
1854 Penny	.75		

LOWER CANADA TOKENS

Date and Description	Buying Price	Date and Description	Buying Price
Magdalen Island	10.00	Pro Bono Publico	1,250.00
Bank Token	1.00	Bank Token Halfpenny	.75
Banque du Peuple, Maple Leaf	1.00	Bank Token Penny	1.00
Banque du Peuple, Wreath	1.00	Bank of Montreal, Sideview Halfpenny	250.00
		Sideview Penny	450.00

LOWER CANADA TOKENS

Date and Description	Buying Price	Date and Description	Buying Price
Montreal Half Penny	2.00	Francis Mullins & Son	3.00
Canada Half Penny	2.00	R.W. Owen	850.00
For Public Accommodation	2.00	J. Shaw & Co.	3.00
T.S. Brown & Co.	2.00	J. Roy	15.00
Ths & Wm Molson	125.00	Agriculture & Commerce	.75

LOWER CANADA TOKENS

Date and Description	Buying Price	Date and Description	Buying Price
Halfpenny Token 1812, Small Wreath	1.00	To Facilitate Trade	
Halfpenny Token 1812, Large Wreath	1.00	Military Bust 1825	2.00
Penny Token 1812	2.00	Civilian Bust 1825	550.00
Victoria Nobis Est	2.00	Spread Eagle	1.00
R H Half Penny	2.00	Halfpenny Token	2.00

LOWER CANADA TOKENS

Date and Description	Buying Price	Date and Description	Buying Price
Seated Justice	1.00	Commercial Change	2.00
Bust/Ships Colonies	1.00	Bust and Harp	1.00

WELLINGTON TOKENS

Date and Description	Buying Price	Date and Description	Buying Price
Field Marshal Wellington	1.00	The Illustrious Wellington	1.00
Marquis Wellington	2.00	Battle Token	1.00

Date and Description	Buying Price	Date and Description	Buying Price
Copper Company	175.00	Success To Commerce	1.00
Lesslie Halfpenny	3.00	Upper & Lower Canada	15.00
Lesslie Twopenny	35.00	Commercial Change 1815	10.00
No Labour No Bread	.75	Commerical Change 1820	1.00
Sir Isaac Brock	.75		

UPPER CANADA TOKENS

Date and Description	Buying Price	Date and Description	Buying Price
Commercial Change 1821		To Facilitate Trade	
Cask Marked Upper Canada	10.00	1823	2.00
Cask Marked Jamaica	200.00	1833	1.00
Province of Upper Canada	5.00	Commercial Change 1833	2.00

PROVINCE OF CANADA TOKENS

89

PROVINCE OF CANADA TOKENS

Date and Description	Buying Price	Date and Description	Buying Price
Bank of Montreal		Quebec Bank, 1852 Halfpenny	.50
1842, 1844 Halfpenny	.50	Penny	1.00
1845 Halfpenny	1,000.00	Bank of Upper Canada 1850-1857	
1837 Penny	50.00	Halfpenny	.50
1842 Penny	1.00	Penny	1.00

ANONYMOUS AND MISCELLANEOUS TOKENS

Date and Description	Buying Price	Date and Description	Buying Price
For General Accommodation	1.00	Pure Copper Preferable	1.00
Success to Trade	10.00	North American	10.00

BRITISH COLUMBIA TOKENS

Date and Description	Buying Price
1802 Pattern Gold $10	25,000.00
1802 Pattern Gold $20	25,000.00

NORTH WEST COMPANY

Date and Description	Buying Price
1820 North West Company Token	200.00

HUDSON'S BAY COMPANY

Date and Description	Buying Price
Hudson's Bay Company Tokens Set of four (1, ½, ¼, 1/8)	30.00

TRANSPORTATION TOKENS

Date and Description	Buying Price
Bridge Tokens, each	40.00
Montreal & Lachine Railroad	20.00

CANADIAN MEDALS

WAR MEDALS 1812 TO 1885

Army
Gold
Cross

Naval
General
Service
Medal

Army
Gold
Medal

Canadian
General
Service
Medal

Army
General
Service
Medal

Egyptian
Medal

Date and Description	Buying Price	Date and Description	Buying Price
Army Gold Cross	15,000.00	Canadian General Service Medal	
Army Gold Medal	5,000.00	Fenian Raid Bar 1866	125.00
Army General Service Medal 1812-1814		Fenian Raid Bar 1870	125.00
Fort Detroit Bar	1,750.00	Red River Bar 1870	500.00
Chateauguay Bar	1,750.00	Egyptian Medal*	
Chrysler's Farm Bar	1,750.00	The Nile Bar	500.00
Naval General Service Medal 1812-1814	150.00	Kirbekan Bar	500.00
		*Awarded to Canadian Boatmen	

WAR MEDALS 1885 TO 1914

Khedive's
Bronze
Star

1914
Star

North West
Canada
Medal

1914-1915
Star

South
Africa
Medal

British
War
Medal

Date and Description	Buying Price	Date and Description	Buying Price
Khedive's Bronze Star	15.00	1914 Star*	750.00
North West Canada Medal 1885	150.00	1914-1915 Star	5.00
Saskatchewan Bar	200.00	British War Medal	8.00
Queen's South Africa			
1899-1900 on reverse	1,750.00		
Dates removed	20.00		
King's South Africa	20.00		

*Canadian Star awarded only to 2nd. Field Hospital.

WAR MEDALS 1914 TO 1945

Allied Victory Medal

The Defence Medal

Merchantile Marine War Medal

WW II 1939-1945 War Medal

Canadian Volunteer Service Medal

Atlantic
Air Crew
Europe
Africa
France and
Germany
Italy
Pacific
Burma

Date and Description	Buying Price
Allied Victory Medal	2.00
Merchantile Marine War Medal	5.00
Canadian Volunteer Service Medal	8.00
Defence Medal	8.00
1939-1945 War Medal	8.00

Date and Description	Buying Price
1939-1945 Star	2.00
Atlantic Star	10.00
Air Crew Europe	50.00
Africa Star	2.00
France and Germany Star	2.00
Italy Star	2.00
Pacific Star	6.00
Burma Star	6.00

WAR MEDALS
1951 TO 1973

COMMEMORATIVE MEDALS

Canadian
Korean
Medal

1911
Coronation
Medal

United
Nations
Korea
Medal

1935
Silver
Jubilee
Medal

United
Nations
Emergency
Medal

1937
Coronation
Medal

Date and Description	Buying Price
Canadian Korean War Medal, English	20.00
Canadian Korean War Medal, French	30.00
United Nations Korea Medal	10.00
United Nations Emergency Medal	10.00
United Nations Medal 1960 to present	10.00
International Commission Medal 1967	10.00
International Commission Medal 1973	10.00

Date and Description	Buying Price
King George V	
Coronation Medal - 1911	15.00
Silver Jubilee Medal - 1935	12.00
King George VI	
Coronation Medal - 1937	12.00

COMMEMORATIVE MEDALS

MEDALS FOR VALOUR AND SERVICE

1953
Coronation
Medal

Victoria
Cross

1977
Silver
Jubilee
Medal

Distinguished
Service
Order

1967
Canadian
Centennial
Medal

Order of
St. Michael
and
St. George

Date and Description	Buying Price	Date and Description	Buying Price
Queen Elizabeth II		Victoria Cross	25,000.00
Coronation Medal - 1953	10.00	Distinguished Service Order	200.00
Silver Jubilee Medal - 1977	35.00	Order of St. Michael and St. George	200.00
Canadian Centennial Medal - 1967	25.00		

MEDALS FOR VALOUR AND SERVICE

Distinguished
Service
Cross

Air
Force
Medal

Distinguished
Flying
Cross

Military
Medal

Air Force
Cross

British
Empire
Medal

Date and Description	Buying Price	Date and Description	Buying Price
Distinguished Service Cross	200.00	Air Force Medal	100.00
Distinguished Flying Cross	300.00	Military Medal	150.00
Air Force Cross	350.00	British Empire Medal	50.00

COINS OF THE UNITED STATES

MINT MARKS

The United State decimal coinage is identified by the following mint marks:

C   -Charlotte, North Carolina
CC -Carson City, Nevada
D   -Dahlonega, Georgia (gold coins only)
D   -Denver, Colorado (1906 to date)
O   -New Orleans, Louisiana
S   -San Francisco, California
P   -Philadelphia, Pennsylvania

HALF CENTS

Liberty Cap

Date and Mint Mark	Buying Price
1793	700.00
1794	100.00
1795	75.00
1796	3,000.00
1797	75.00

Draped Bust

Date and Mint Mark	Buying Price
1800	15.00
1802	250.00
1803-1808	15.00

Classic Head

Date and Mint Mark	Buying Price
1809-1810	12.50
1811	60.00
1825 to 1835	10.00

Coronet Head

Date and Mint Mark	Buying Price
1849 to 1857	15.00

LARGE CENTS

Flowing Hair

Date and Mint Mark	Buying Price
1793	700.00

Liberty Cap

Date and Mint Mark	Buying Price
1793	1,000.00
1794	75.00
1795	40.00
1796	50.00

Draped Bust

Date and Mint Mark	Buying Price
1796	50.00
1797	20.00
1798	15.00
1799	500.00
1800 to 1803	10.00
1804	200.00
1805 to 1807	10.00

Classic Head

Date and Mint Mark	Buying Price
1808	10.00
1809	30.00
1810	10.00
1811	20.00
1812 to 1814	10.00

Coronet Head

Date and Mint Mark	Buying Price
1816 to 1820	4.00
1821	10.00
1822	4.00
1823	15.00
1824 to 1838	4.00
1839 to 1856	3.00
1857	10.00

SMALL CENTS

Flying Eagle

Date and Mint Mark	Buying Price
1856	1,250.00
1857 to 1859	6.00

Indian Head

Date and Mint Mark	Buying Price
1860 to 1865	1.25
1866 to 1868	10.00
1869 to 1872	14.00
1873 to 1876	4.00
1877	175.00
1878	10.00
1879 to 1886	.75
1887 to 1908	.40
1908S	12.00
1909	.40
1909S	100.00

Lincoln Head Wheat Ears

Date and Mint Mark	Buying Price
1909	.10
1909VDB	.50
1909S	15.00
1909S VDB	150.00
1910 to 1914	.10
1914D	35.00
1915D to 1931D	.10
1931S	14.00
1932 to 1958	.01
1955 Double Die	150.00

Lincoln Head Memorial

Date and Mint Mark	Buying Price
1955 to 2000	.01

TWO CENTS

Date and Mint Mark	Buying Price
1864 to 1871	2.50
1872	20.00
1873 Proof	400.00

THREE CENTS

Silver

Date and Mint Mark	Buying Price
1851 to 1862	5.00
1863 to 1873 Proof	50.00

Nickel

Date and Mint Mark	Buying Price
1865 to 1874	3.00
1875 to 1876	4.00
1877 to 1878 Proof	200.00
1879 to 1880	20.00
1881	3.00
1882	25.00
1883	50.00
1884 to 1887	125.00
1888 to 1889	20.00

FIVE CENTS NICKEL

Shield

Date and Mint Mark	Buying Price
1866 to 1870	3.00
1871	10.00
1872 to 1878	4.00
1879 to 1881	75.00
1882 to 1883	3.00

Liberty Head

Date and Mint Mark	Buying Price
1883 to 1884	1.25
1885	75.00
1886	30.00
1887 to 1896	1.00
1897 to 1912D	.50
1912S	20.00

Indian Head or Buffalo Type

Date and Mint Mark	Buying Price
1913	1.50
1914 to 1918	.50
1918D 8/7	150.00
1919 to 1938	.25

Jefferson Type

Date and Mint Mark	Buying Price
1938 to 2000	.05

HALF DIMES

Flowing Hair

Date and Mint Mark	Buying Price
1794	225.00
1795	225.00

Draped Bust

Date and Mint Mark	Buying Price
1796 to 1797	300.00
1800 to 1801	175.00
1802	3,000.00
1803 to 1805	150.00

Capped Bust

Date and Mint Mark	Buying Price
1829 to 1837	7.00

Liberty Seated

Date and Mint Mark	Buying Price
1837	12.00
1838 No Stars	30.00
1838 to 1845	3.50
1846	50.00
1847 to 1863	3.50
1864	90.00
1864S	12.00
1865	75.00
1866	60.00
1866S	8.00
1867	125.00
1867S	8.00
1868 to 1873	3.00

DIMES

Draped Bust

Date and Mint Mark	Buying Price
1796 to 1797	600.00
1798 to 1807	200.00

Capped Bust

Date and Mint Mark	Buying Price
1809 to 1811	30.00
1814 to 1821	7.00
1822	150.00
1823 to 1837	7.00

Liberty Seated

Date and Mint Mark	Buying Price
1837 to 1838 No stars	15.00
1839 to 1840O	2.00
1840	15.00
1841 to 1843	2.00
1843O and 1844	15.00
1845	2.00
1846	25.00
1847 to 1856	3.00
1856S	20.00
1857 to 1860	2.00
1858S	20.00
1859S	35.00
1860O	150.00
1861 and 1862	3.00
1863	60.00
1864 to 1867	50.00
1864S to 1867S	5.00
1868 to 1874	3.00
1871CC	200.00
1872CC	100.00
1873CC No Arrows	Unique
1874CC	600.00
1875 to 1878	2.00
1878CC	2.50
1879	50.00
1880 to 1881	40.00
1882 to 1885	2.00
1885S	100.00
1886 to 1891	2.00

Barber

Date and Mint Mark	Buying Price
1892 to 1895	1.50
1895O	200.00
1896O	40.00
1897 to 1916	.40

Mercury Head

Date and Mint Mark	Buying Price
1916	.45
1916D	250.00
1917 to 1945	.45

Roosevelt - Silver

Date and Mint Mark	Buying Price
1946 to 1964	.45

Roosevelt - Clad

Date and Mint Mark	Buying Price
1965 to 2000	.10

TWENTY CENTS

Date and Mint Mark	Buying Price
1875 to 1876	25.00
1877 to 1878	200.00

QUARTER DOLLAR

Draped Bust

Date and Mint Mark	Buying Price
1796	2,000.00
1804	350.00
1805 to 1807	75.00

Capped Bust

Date and Mint Mark	Buying Price
1815 to 1822	20.00
1823/2	3,000.00
1824 to 1828	15.00
1831 to 1838 Reduced Size	15.00

Liberty Seated

Date and Mint Mark	Buying Price
1838 to 1849	5.00
1849O	175.00
1850 to 1851	10.00
1851O	75.00
1852	15.00
1852O	85.00

Date and Mint Mark	Buying Price
1853 to 1862	5.00
1862S to 1864	10.00
1864S	75.00
1865 to 1870	20.00
1870CC	500.00
1871CC	400.00
1871S	100.00
1872CC	150.00
1872S	100.00
1871 to 1878CC	4.00
1878S to 1888	30.00
1888S	4.00
1889 and 1890	20.00
1891O	40.00
1891 and 1891S	4.00

Barber

Date and Mint Mark	Buying Price
1892 to 1896	1.10
1896S	125.00
1897 to 1901	1.10
1901S	750.00
1902 to 1913	1.10
1913S	200.00
1914 to 1916	1.10

Standing Liberty

Date and Mint Mark	Buying Price
1916	500.00
1917 to 1930	1.10

Washington - Silver

Date and Mint Mark	Buying Price
1932 to 1964	1.10

Washington - Clad

Date and Mint Mark	Buying Price
1965 to 1975	.25

200th Bi-Centennial

Date and Mint Mark	Buying Price
1976	.25

Washington - Clad

Date and Mint Mark	Buying Price
1977 to 2000	.25

Note: Coins must be in very good condition or better to command these prices, coins grading good or less will sell at lower prices.

HALF DOLLARS
Flowing Hair

Date and Mint Mark	Buying Price
1794	600.00
1795	175.00

Draped Bust

Date and Mint Mark	Buying Price
1796 15 Stars	4,000.00
1796 16 Stars	4,000.00
1797 15 Stars	4,000.00
1801 to 1802	50.00
1803 to 1807	30.00

Capped Bust

Date and Mint Mark	Buying Price
1807	15.00
1808 to 1814	10.00

Date and Mint Mark	Buying Price
1815	300.00
1817 to 1836	12.00
1836 Reeded Edge	250.00
1837 to 1839	15.00
1839O	60.00

Liberty Seated

Date and Mint Mark	Buying Price
1839 to 1852O	8.00
1850	50.00
1851	50.00
1852	75.00
1853O	5,000.00
1853 to 1855	8.00
1855S Arrows	150.00
1856 to 1865S	7.00
1866 to 1873CC	5.00
1870CC	200.00
1873 to 1874S	15.00
1875 to 1878	5.00
1878CC	100.00
1878S	2,000.00
1879 to 1890	50.00
1891	8.00

Barber

Date and Mint Mark	Buying Price
1892	8.00
1892O and 1892S	40.00
1893 to 1897	3.00
1897O	20.00
1897S	35.00
1898 to 1915	2.00

Liberty Walking

Date and Mint Mark	Buying Price
1916 to 1920	2.25
1921	30.00
1921D	35.00
1923 to 1947	2.25

Franklin

Date and Mint Mark	Buying Price
1948 to 1963	2.25

Kennedy - Silver

Date and Mint Mark	Buying Price
1964	2.25

Kennedy - Silver Clad

Date and Mint Mark	Buying Price
1965 to 1970	1.00

Kennedy - Copper Clad

Date and Mint Mark	Buying Price
1971 to 1998	.50

SILVER DOLLARS

Flowing Hair

Date and Mint Mark	Buying Price
1794	3,500.00
1795	300.00

Draped Bust

Date and Mint Mark	Buying Price
1795	250.00
1796 to 1798	250.00
1798 to 1803	100.00

Note: Coins must grade very good (VG) or better to command prices listed.

Liberty Seated

Date and Mint Mark	Buying Price
1840 to 1873	35.00
1851 and 1852	300.00
1858	400.00
1870CC	100.00
1870S	20,000.00
1871CC	750.00
1872CC	300.00
1872S	75.00
1873CC	900.00

Liberty Head

Date and Mint Mark	Buying Price
1878 to 1892	5.00
1878CC to 1881CC	13.00
1882CC to 1884CC	15.00
1885CC	75.00
1889CC	125.00
1893CC	125.00
1890O to 1893O	5.00
1893S	500.00
1894	100.00
1895O	65.00
1895S	80.00
1896 to 1903	5.00
1903O	50.00
1904 to 1921	5.00

Peace

Date and Mint Mark	Buying Price
1921 to 1927	6.00
1928	35.00
1928S to 1935	6.00

Eisenhower

Date and Mint Mark	Buying Price
1971 to 1976	1.00

Susan B. Anthony

Date and Mint Mark	Buying Price
1979 to 1981	1.00

TRADE DOLLARS

Date and Mint Mark	Buying Price
1873 to 1878	25.00
1878CC	75.00

GOLD DOLLARS

Type 1 Liberty Head

Date and Mint Mark	Buying Price
1849 to 1854	75.00

Type 2 Indian Head, Small

Date and Mint Mark	Buying Price
1854 to 1855	100.00
1855C	350.00
1855D	700.00

Type 3 Indian Head, Large

Date and Mint Mark	Buying Price
1856 to 1889	75.00
1856D	500.00
1860D	400.00
1861D	1,000.00
1875	375.00

GOLD 2 ½ DOLLARS

Capped Bust Right

Date and Mint Mark	Buying Price
1796	2,000.00
1797 to 1807	600.00

Capped Bust Left

Date and Mint Mark	Buying Price
1808	2,000.00

Capped Head Left

Date and Mint Mark	Buying Price
1821 to 1827	600.00
1829 to 1833	500.00
1834 (motto)	1,250.00

Classic Head

Date and Mint Mark	Buying Price
1834 to 1839	100.00

Coronet Head

Date and Mint Mark	Buying Price
1840 to 1907	90.00
1848 California	2,000.00
1854D	500.00
1854S	12,500.00
1855D	350.00
1856D	450.00
1875	250.00

Indian Head

Date and Mint Mark	Buying Price
1908 to 1929	100.00
1911D	150.00

3 DOLLARS

Date and Mint Mark	Buying Price
1854 to 1873	300.00
1854D	750.00
1873 Closed 3	300.00
1880 to 1889	300.00

4 DOLLARS

Date and Mint Mark	Buying Price
1879 to 1880	6,000.00

GOLD 5 DOLLARS

Capped Bust Right

Date and Mint Mark	Buying Price
1795 to 1797	2,000.00
1798 to 1807	300.00

Draped Bust Left

Date and Mint Mark	Buying Price
1807 to 1834	500.00
1821	350.00
1822	12,500.00
1823	250.00
1824	750.00
1825	750.00
1826	450.00
1827	650.00
1828	750.00
1829	750.00

Classic Head

Date and Mint Mark	Buying Price
1834 to 1838	125.00
1838C	175.00
1838D	175.00

Coronet Head

Date and Mint Mark	Buying Price
1839 to 1908	115.00
1842C Small Date	250.00
1854S	12,500.00
1861C	250.00
1861D	500.00
1864S	150.00
1865	135.00
1870CC	225.00
1875	1,250.00
1878CC	200.00

Indian Head

Date and Mint Mark	Buying Price
1908 to 1916	125.00
1929	350.00

GOLD 10 DOLLARS

Capped Bust Right

Date and Mint Mark	Buying Price
Small Eagle, 1795 to 1797	1,000.00
Heraldic Eagle, 1797 to 1803	600.00

Coronet Head

Date and Mint Mark	Buying Price
1838 to 1907	250.00
1858	500.00
1859O	300.00
1859S	250.00
1863	325.00
1864S	500.00
1865S	275.00
1866S	275.00
1870CC	300.00
1873	300.00
1873CC	300.00
1875 Proof	4,000.00
1876	300.00
1877	300.00
1877CC	300.00
1878CC	300.00
1879CC	300.00
1879O	250.00
1883O	200.00

$10 Indian Head

Date and Mint Mark	Buying Price
1907 to 1932	250.00
1920S	500.00
1930S	300.00
1933	5,000.00

GOLD $20 DOLLARS

Liberty

Date and Mint Mark	Buying Price
1850 to 1907	450.00
1854O	2,500.00
1855O	600.00
1856O	2,500.00
1859O	600.00
1860O	600.00
1861O	500.00
1870CC	3,000.00
1871CC	500.00
1879O	600.00
1881	650.00
1882	700.00
1885	650.00
1886	1,000.00
1891	600.00
1891CC	500.00

$20 St. Gaudens

Date and Mint Mark	Buying Price
1907 MCMVII	800.00
1907 to 1916	450.00
1920S	1,000.00
1921	2,000.00
1922 to 1928	450.00
1927D	12,500.00
1927S	600.00
1929	750.00
1930 to 1932	1,000.00

GOLD COMMEMORATIVE COINS

Date and Mint Mark	Buying Price
1903 $1 Louisiana Purchase	150.00
1904-05 $1 Lewis & Clark Exposition	250.00
1915S $1 Panama-Pacific Exposition	150.00
1916 $1 McKinley Memorial	150.00
1917 $1 McKinley Memorial	175.00
1922 $1 Grant Memorial, With Star	450.00
1922 $1 Grant Memorial, Without Star	400.00
1915S $2.50 Panama-Pacific Exposition	500.00
1926 $2.50 Philadelphia Sesquicentennial	100.00
1984P and D $10 Olympic	200.00
1984S $10 Olympic	200.00
1984W $10 Olympic	200.00
1986W $5 Liberty	100.00
1987W $5 Constitution	100.00
1988W $5 Oylmpic	100.00
1989W $5 Congress	100.00
1991W $5 Mount Rushmore	100.00
1992W $5 Olympic	100.00
1992W $5 Columbus	100.00
1993W $5 Bill of Rights	100.00
1993W $5 WWII	100.00
1994W $5 World Cup	100.00
1995 W $5 Civil War	100.00
1995W $5 Olympic Torch	100.00
1995W $5 Olympic Stadium	100.00
1996W $5 Flag Bearer	100.00
1996W $5 Cauldron	100.00
1996W $5 Smithsonian	100.00
1997W $5 F.D.R.	100.00

WORLD GOLD COINS

This partial listing of world gold coins indicates the prices dealers are willing to pay based on the Canadian dollar gold price as at May 24th, 1999. Prices will fluctuate with the market price of gold, plus the Canadian-U.S. dollar exchange rate.

AUSTRIA

Date and Denom.	Fine Gold Content Oz.	Buying Price
1912 10K	0.0980	35.00
1915 20K	0.1960	70.00
1915 100K	0.9803	350.00
1915 1D	0.1109	40.00
1914 4D	0.4438	158.00
1892 10Fr	0.0933	33.00
1892 20Fr*	0.1867	67.00

BAHAMAS

Date and Denom.	Fine Gold Content Oz.	Buying Price
1967 $10	0.1177	42.00
1971 $10	0.1177	42.00
1972 $10	0.0940	34.00
1967 $20	0.2355	84.00
1971 $20*	0.2355	84.00
1972 $20	0.1880	67.00
1967 $50	0.5888	210.00
1971 $50	0.5888	210.00
1972 $50	0.4708	108.00
1967 $100	1.1776	420.00
1971 $100	1.1776	420.00
1972 $100	0.9420	336.00

* Coin illustrated

BELGIUM

Date and Denom.	Fine Gold Content Oz.	Buying Price
1867 to 1914 20Fr	0.1867	67.00

BERMUDA

Date and Denom.	Fine Gold Content Oz.	Buying Price
1970 $20	0.2355	84.00
1977 $50	0.1172	42.00
1975 $100*	0.2304	82.00
1977 $100	0.2344	82.00

CAYMAN ISLANDS

Date and Denom.	Fine Gold Content Oz.	Buying Price
1972 $25*	0.2532	90.00
1974 $50	0.1823	65.00
1974 $100	0.3646	130.00
1975 $100	0.3646	130.00
1977 $100	0.3464	124.00

CHILE

Date and Denom.	Fine Gold Content Oz.	Buying Price
1898 to 1900 5p	0.0883	31.50
1896 to 1901 10p*	0.1766	63.00
1896 to 1917 20p	0.3532	126.00
1926 to 1980 100p	0.5886	210.00

COLUMBIA

Date and Denom.	Fine Gold Content Oz.	Buying Price
1913 to 1929 2 ½ p	0.1177	42.00
1913 to 1930 5p	0.2355	84.00
1919 and 1924 10p	0.4710	168.00
1973 1500p*	0.5527	197.00

FRANCE

Date and Denom.	Fine Gold Content Oz.	Buying Price
1856 to 1869 5Fr	0.0467	17.00
1854 to 1914 10Fr	0.0933	33.50
1809 to 1914 20Fr*	0.1867	67.00
1810 to 1838 40Fr	0.3734	134.00
1855 to 1864 50Fr	0.4667	167.00
1855 to 1913 100Fr	0.9335	335.00

GERMANY

Date and Denom.	Fine Gold Content Oz.	Buying Price
1872 to 1914 10DM	0.1152	41.00
1871 to 1914 20DM*	0.2304	82.00

GREAT BRITAIN

Date and Denom.	Fine Gold Content Oz.	Buying Price
1863 to 1915 ½ Sov.	0.1177	42.00
1871 to 1968 Sov.*	0.2354	84.00
1887 Two Pound	0.4708	168.00
1897 Two Pound	0.4708	168.00
1902 Two Pound	0.4708	168.00
1911 Two Pound	0.4708	168.00
1937 Two Pound	0.4708	168.00
1887 Five Pound	1.1773	420.00
1897 Five Pound	1.1773	420.00
1902 Five Pound	1.1773	420.00
1911 Five Pound	1.1773	420.00
1937 Five Pound	1.1773	420.00

IRAN

Date and Denom.	Fine Gold Content Oz.	Buying Price
1971 500R	0.1883	67.00
1971 750R*	0.2827	100.00
1971 1000R	0.3770	134.00
1971 2000R	0.7541	268.00

* Coin illustrated

ITALY

Date and Denom.	Fine Gold Content Oz.	Buying Price
1932 to 1860 10L	0.0931	33.00
1831 to 1860 20L*	0.1867	66.00
1822 to 1831 40L	0.3733	132.00
1832 to 1844 100L	0.9332	330.00

NETHERLANDS

Date and Denom.	Fine Gold Content Oz.	Buying Price
1900 to 1937 1D*	0.1109	40.00
1912 5G	0.0973	35.00
1875 to 1933 10G	0.1947	69.00

JAMAICA

Date and Denom.	Fine Gold Content Oz.	Buying Price
1972 $20*	0.2531	90.00
1975, 1976 $100	0.2265	81.00
1978 $100	0.3281	117.00
1978, 1979 $250	1.2507	446.00

PANAMA

Date and Denom.	Fine Gold Content Oz.	Buying Price
1975 to 1979 100B*	0.2361	84.00
1975 to 1979 500B	1.2067	430.00

MEXICO

Date and Denom.	Fine Gold Content Oz.	Buying Price
1945 2p	0.0482	17.00
1945 2 1/2p	0.0602	21.00
1955 5p	0.1205	43.00
1959 10p*	0.2411	86.00
1959 20p	0.4823	172.00
1947 50p	1.2057	430.00

Above dates are restrikes.

RUSSIA

Date and Denom.	Fine Gold Content Oz.	Buying Price
1897 to 1911 5R*	0.1244	44.00
1897 7 1/2R	0.1867	67.00
1898 to 1911 10R	0.2489	89.00
1897 15R	0.3734	133.00
1977 to 1988 100R	0.5000	178.00

IMPORTANT: Buying prices are listed for coins graded VF or better. Bent, damaged or badly worn coins are worth less.

*Coin Illustrated

APPENDIX

BULLION VALUES

Silver and gold coins and other numismatic items are often bought by dealers for their bullion value, that is the value of the pure precious metals which they contain. The weight of precious metals is expressed in grams or troy ounces, not in avoirdupois ounces. A troy ounce is greater than an avoirdupois ounce.

1 Troy Ounce = 31.21035 Grams
1 Avoirdupois Ounce = 28.349 Grams

GOLD

The quanitity of pure gold in gold coins is calculated by multiplying the gold fineness or purity of the coin by its weight in troy ounces or grams. Gold purity can also be expressed in karats, a 24-part system with 24-karats equalling pure gold, 22 karats equalling 22 parts gold to 2 parts base metal, 18 karats equalling 18 parts gold to 6 parts base metal etc.

Karats	Fineness	Purity
24	.999	99.9%
22	.916	91.6%
18	.750	75.0%
14	.585	58.5%
10	.417	41.7%
9	.375	37.5%

1 14-karat or .585 fine gold coin weighing 1 troy ounce contains 1 ounce x .585 = .585 troy ounces of pure gold. If gold is worth $600 per troy ounce, then this coin is worth $600 x .585 = $351. (See extended charts on following pages.)

SILVER

The quantity of pure silver in silver coins is calculated by multiplying the silver fineness or purity of the coin by its weight in troy ounces.

Karats	Fineness	Purity
Pure	.999	99.9%
Fine	.999	99.9%
Sterling	.925	92.5%
Coin	.800	80.0%
Coin	.500	50.0%

A .800 fine silver coin weighing 1 troy ounce contains 1 x .800 = .800 troy ounces of pure silver. If silver is worth $20 an ounce, then this coin is worth $20 x .800 = $16. (See extended charts on following pages.)

GOLD CONTENT OF CANADIAN GOLD COIN

Denom.	Date and Mint Mark	Gross Weight (Grams)	Fineness	Pure Gold Content Grams	Troy Oz.
1 pd.	1908C-1910C	7.99	.917	7.32	.236
1 pd.	1911C-1919C	7.99	.917	7.32	.236
$2	1865-1888	3.33	.917	3.05	.100
$5	1912-1914	8.36	.900	7.52	.242
$10	1912-1914	16.72	.900	15.05	.484
$20	1967	18.27	.900	16.45	.529
$5 M.L.	1982 to date	3.11	.9999	3.11	.10
$10 M.L.	1982 to date	7.78	.9999	7.78	.25
$20 M.L.	1986 to date	15.57	.9999	15.57	.500
$50 M.L.	1979 to date	31.10	.999	31.10	1.000
$100	1976 (Unc.)	13.33	.583	7.78	.250
$100	1976 (Proof)	16.96	.917	15.55	.499
$100	1977-1986	16.96	.917	15.55	.499
$100	1987 to date	13.33	.583	7.78	.250
$175	1992	16.97	.916	15.544	.500
$200	1990 to date	17.106	.916	15.669	.500
$350	1998 to date	38.05	.9999	38.050	1.223

SILVER CONTENT OF CANADIAN SILVER COINS

Denom.	Date	Fineness	Silver Content Grams	Troy Oz.
$20	1985-1988	.925	31.103	1.000
$10	1973-1976	.925	44.955	1.445
$5	1973-1976	.925	22.477	.723
$5 M.L.	1987 to date	.999	31.103	1.000
$1	1935-1967	.800	18.661	.600
$1	1971 to date	.500	11.662	.375
50-cents	1870-1919	.925	10.792	.347
50-cents	1920-1967	.800	9.330	.300
25-cents	1870-1919	.925	5.370	.173
25-cents	1920-1967	.800	4.665	.150
25-cents	1967-1968	.500	2.923	.094
10-cents	1858-1919	.925	2.146	.069
10-cents	1920-1967	.800	1.866	.060
10-cents	1967-1968	.500	1.170	.038
5-cents	1858-1919	.925	1.080	.034
5-cents	1920-1921	.800	.933	.030

PLATINUM CONTENT OF CANADIAN PLATINUM COINS

Denom.	Date	Fineness	Platinum Content Grams	Troy Oz.
$300	1990-2000	.9999	31.1	1.000
$150	1990-2000	.9999	15.6	.500
$75	1990-2000	.9999	7.8	.250
$30	1990-2000	.9999	3.1	.100

BULLION VALUES OF CANADIAN GOLD COINS

Computed from $300 to $700 per troy ounce in increments of $100 Canadian.

Denom.	Date and Mint Mark	$300	$400	$500	$600	$700
1 pd.	1908C-1910C	70.95	94.40	118.00	141.60	165.20
1 pd.	1911C-1919C	70.95	94.40	118.00	141.60	165.20
$2	1865-1888	30.00	40.00	50.00	60.00	70.00
$5	1912-1914	72.60	96.60	121.00	145.20	160.40
$10	1912-1914	145.20	193.60	242.00	290.40	338.00
$20	1967	15.70	211.60	264.50	317.40	370.30
$5 M.L.	1982 to date	30.00	40.00	50.00	60.00	70.00
$10 M.L.	1982 to date	75.00	100.00	125.00	150.00	175.00
$20 M.L.	1986 to date	150.00	200.00	250.00	300.00	350.00
$50 M.L.	1979 to date	300.00	400.00	500.00	600.00	700.00
$100	1976 (Unc)	75.00	100.00	125.00	150.00	175.00
$100	1976 (Proof)	150.00	200.00	250.00	300.00	350.00
$100	1977-1986	150.00	200.00	250.00	300.00	350.00
$100	1987 (Proof)	75.00	100.00	125.00	150.00	175.00

BULLION VALUES OF CANADIAN SILVER COINS

Computed from $5 to $50 per troy ounce in increments of $10 Canadian.

Denom.	Fineness	$5	$10	$20	$30	$40	$50
$20	.925	5.00	10.00	20.00	30.00	40.00	50.00
$10	.925	7.23	14.00	28.90	43.35	57.80	72.15
$5	.925	3.62	7.23	14.46	21.69	28.92	36.15
$5 M.L.	.999	5.00	10.00	20.00	30.00	40.00	50.00
$1	.800	3.00	6.00	12.00	18.00	24.00	30.00
$1	.500	1.88	3.75	7.50	11.25	15.00	18.75
50 cents	.925	1.74	3.47	6.94	10.41	13.88	17.35
50 cents	.800	1.50	3.00	6.00	9.00	12.00	15.00
25 cents	.925	.87	1.73	3.46	5.19	6.92	8.65
25 cents	.800	.75	1.50	3.00	4.50	6.00	7.50
25 cents	.500	.47	.94	1.88	2.82	3.76	4.70
10 cents	.925	.35	.69	1.38	2.07	2.76	3.45
10 cents	.800	.30	.60	1.20	1.80	2.40	3.00
10 cents	.500	.19	.38	.76	1.14	1.52	1.90
5 cents	.925	.17	.34	.68	1.02	1.36	1.70
5-cents	.800	.15	.30	.60	.90	1.20	1.50